UP NORTH

by

Dick Case

Oh, How Upstate©
Enterprises
Liverpool, New York
www.OhHowUpstate.com

Published by Oh, How Upstate© Enterprises, 200 Old Liverpool Road,
Liverpool, NY 13088
(315) 478-1122 ext.17. First edition.
books@rivette.us
www.OhHowUpstate.com

ISBN 0-9744046-5-9

LCCN 2007933631

First printing: October 2007

Writing by Dick Case
Photography by Daniel Coon and David Lassman;
Computer assistance by Jan Dempsey

Layout and production by United Imaging and Printing,
Syracuse, NY

DEDICATION

To Elizabeth, Jonathan and Laurel

An Introduction

I have always been fascinated by words – their history, their magic and their power. I believe I probably share that with the person I am about to introduce.

Because of this I tend to love dictionaries, and with the Internet I'm in heaven whenever I want to look up the source or meaning of a word. When writing this, I thought I would select a word that I think best describes him, and examine its true meaning. For me, that word would truly be "curious".

Quite simply, *curious* is defined as beyond or deviating from the usual or expected; eager to investigate (sometimes about others' concerns); and being eagerly interested in learning more. Its archaic definition also means "accomplished with skill or ingenuity" and "extremely careful; scrupulous."

Curious is also a description of a type of glass that did not meet the manufacturer's specifications. Mostly this glass is very unusual, unpredictable, sometimes beautiful and sometimes ugly.

Britney Spears, by the way, named her perfume "Curious." (What, you might ask, does Britney Spears have to do with this person I introduce to you? Not a thing – I just thought it was a curious connection.)

However, all of the various meanings of the word describe this man and his life work. I have known him ever since I moved to Syracuse in 1990, although I never met him until several years ago. Along with a number of people throughout Central New York I have enjoyed his passion for ideas, his curiosity about people, his concern for social justice, and his ability to tell stories. Give him a problem and he will do his best to solve it. Show him an injustice and he will work to expose the problem. He pulls no punches and keeps all of us in this town honest.

I especially like the description of "curious glass". For Dick Case, in his newspaper column, finds the unusual, the unpredictable, the beautiful and yes, sometimes the ugly. But his curiosity always illuminates. By the way, the great Dorothy Parker once said "*The cure for boredom is curiosity. There is no cure for curiosity.*"

- Heide Holtz, introducing Dick Case at a
Rosamond Gifford Foundation event, 2006.

Foreword

For most of us in Central New York, when we say *Up North* the compass spins toward the upland of the state north of the Thruway. It's a broad landscape that reaches the St. Lawrence River, the Adirondacks, Tug Hill and Lake Ontario, and lots of stops through the middle.

It's close in distance, close to the heart. We love to roam it. The territory's a challenge.

This collection of columns from the Post-Standard, my present employer, and the Herald-Journal-American, my old one, is the next step in an adventure I started in 1994 with the publication of *Good Guys, Bad Guys, Big Guys, Little Guys.* Back then, I paused mid-career and assembled some of my favorite pieces that had a shelf life. The book held 105 columns.

Putting *Good Guys* together was almost as much fun as seeing it in print. I prowled a stack of more that 3,000 columns, wearing out my fingers and eyes but kicking in a lot of memories, most of them pleasant.

I got the same boot this time, back for a second date with folks such as the Old Whittler, Ray Fadden, Dud Frasure, the Bird family, Seth Moulton, and the Scott Brothers.

Not to forget the memorable landscapes I discovered for myself: the Grandmother Tree, Mike's Cabin, Onchiota, Wolfe Island, The Dunes and Our Prairie.

I've narrowed the focus *Up North.*

It's probably a boast without paper work, but I think I have the best job in town. How else would I have had these priceless encounters?

I guess the book is the paperwork.

All of these portraits were painted from life, close-up and comfortable. They've got a lot of miles on them.

Journalists are story-tellers who search, collect and share. It's an open-ended quest. I'm still at it.

– *Dick Case, Syracuse, 2007.*

The Chapters

Our Wild North

There are two thresholds in the Adirondack Mountains of New York. One is literal. When you get above 4,000-feet elevation, the spruce lie flat against the rocks. You aren't in New York anymore; you are in an Arctic clime.

The sun might be shining on the flats while a blizzard slaps around the high peaks.

Bill Sussdorff is a district ranger in the High Peaks region. He has been involved in hundreds of searches and rescues. These average 100 a year in the Adirondacks. Most of the time people get lost and die because of stupid mistakes in judgment.

"They went over the threshold," Bill pointed out.

They climbed too high when they shouldn't have climbed at all. Then they did something foolish. Such as heading on alone, or panicking and losing the native sense of where they were. Or failing to bring the right clothing and equipment.

"Most people don't realize what it's like up here," he explained. "They don't realize the dangers of that elevation. Above the tree line (4,000 feet), there's an eco-system all its own. Down below you can be having nice fall weather, and it's the Arctic on the top. That's when we get people lost and killed. It's kind of fickle."

"Yes," Bill said, "April and October are the most treacherous times."

The years are filled with stories of successful searches and rescues. Bill's employer, the state Department of Environmental Conservation, is responsible for these on New York's wild lands. Unfortunately for the balance of history, the failures are the ones we remember.

Robert Thomas went up Mount Marcy, our highest peak, about 10 years ago. He was with friends from the Mohawk Valley. It was April, and a blizzard took over the upper quarter of the mountain. He has never been found.

"They still have a poster of him at Adirondack Lodge in Placid," Ranger Dave Ames told me. "Members of his family have gone up looking for him over the years. He just disappeared."

Some day someone ought to draw up a list of these Adirondack mysteries. Hunters, climbers, hikers, fishers, trappers and tourists who went into the woods and "just disappeared."

Dave Ames helped look for the young man on Marcy. "It was extreme weather, snow and high winds," he said. "I believe there were three of them and they stopped at a lean-to called Plateau, which is about 4,000 feet. His buddies wanted to wait, but Thomas wanted to get to the top. He started out and got tangled up somehow."

Rangers weren't notified for two days. By that time the blizzard had buried any trail there might have been. Things were so bad — Arctic topside and spring floods downside —

that only helicopters could be used. Bill Sussdorff was in charge of that search.

"Their mistake was not turning back when they saw how bad the weather was," he said. "And Thomas shouldn't have separated himself from the others. He literally disappeared off the face of the earth. We looked for him for a month before we gave up."

Three years later family and friends were still looking. What they found was the skeleton of another hiker, George Atkinson. He had vanished the same spring.

The classic Adirondack missing person is Dougie Legg of Baldwinsville. Dougie is the other one the rangers talk about when you get them on the subject of the tragic, frustrating part of their jobs.

We searched and searched for Dougie during the summer of 1971 and 1972. He was 8 years old when he wandered out of sight at his family's summer place on Newcomb Lake. Not a hair of the child was ever found. The experts figure he fell into one of those cracks in the rocky forest floor.

This isn't strange to a veteran ranger like Morgan Roderick. "This is very rugged country," he explained. "After a period of time, there's nothing to find."

Sometimes the police are called: There may be a crime. State Police Investigator Frank Dunning works out of Gouveneur. He has 19 years as a trooper and many more as a hunter, fisherman and trapper in the Adirondacks.

It was Frank who told me how inexperience can kill.

Or at least cause you to lose it for a while.

He also mentioned that there are certain people — one being the city resident who leaves his yard once a year to go hunting — who should never step outside a car in a wilderness as mean as our North Woods.

"Inexperience, that's the problem," Frank said. "People think they're lost, and they're so afraid they go wild. They're afraid of the woods and the dark. When you try to help them, they run from you. They hide. They really lose it."

So what does this hunter-trapper-trooper's experience tell him?

"If you're going in, take a map and a compass," Frank continued. "And believe the compass. I think a short survival course should be made a part of the license process. It should be mandatory.

"Don't drop your gun and run if you think you're lost. Don't go crazy and run around. Sit down and wait!"

Among the real tragedies of the Adirondacks are a few stories of people who seem to be missing but aren't. Some were hoaxes. Like the hiker rangers were searching for near Lake George while he was sitting in Florida. Later he confessed to a priest, but many hours were wasted.

Or the greenhorns who think it will be great pretending they are back to basics in the forest preserve until they have to deal with black flies, cold nights, thunder and lightning.

Frank Dunning has a case like that right now, in fact. He can't close it, but he knows he hasn't got a missing naturalist. For about a month last spring, he thought so, though.

A camp site was discovered May 17 by a group of young men who live near Wegatchie, southwest of Gouveneur. When they came back a few days later, it was exactly the same. A .22 leaned against a tree. There were backpacks, a tarp, ammo, clothing, food, an ax and a diary with entries in red ink.

One of them read: "*We cant all lead lives of advenshure but somebody has to do it. This is my first day in the Adirondac Mountains...*" That was dated May 10. The only other entry had been made May 11. "*Living off the land is not easy,*" the diarist wrote.

The rangers were called, and they started to search. One challenge was that they didn't know whom they were searching for. Frank Dunning hiked in and checked the baggage tickets on luggage. It seemed the naturalist had taken an early May flight from Florida to Syracuse. He also started checking area stores because most of the camping gear looked new; some it still had prices tags on it.

When the ground searches and the store searches got them nowhere, the searchers asked the press for help. A newspaper story produced a call to Frank from a young man who identified himself as Dave Donahue of Fulton.

"He said he knew the guy we were looking for," Frank said. "In fact, he had taken him up there and dropped him off."

The missing man was identified as Steve Swanz, 34, of Sarasota, Florida. And where is Steve now? In Sarasota,

Florida, according to Frank.

"His friend verified he's there," the trooper explained. "We turned over the gear to him. We asked Donahue to ask him to get in touch with us, but he hasn't yet. We also asked the sheriff's department down there to find him but so far they haven't been able to, because of his life-style. We know he's alive." - *1987*

The Old Whittler

Ray Dann is the man who whittles chains from single sticks of wood. Some of these wonders are 6 or 7 feet long.

Much of the work is done with a jackknife; not a drop of glue is used. Ray's whittling is continuous, like the ongoing peel of an apple that produces a graceful, single spiral of red skin. The links — sometimes they are very small — are made more interesting by balls and hearts in cages and false interlocks.

Ray is a retired truck mechanic who left Syracuse 20 years ago and placed his trailer on two acres of Oswego County west of Hastings. The little settlement at the edge of the woods, where Ray whittles, is called Catfish Corners. He was born at Genoa.

Ray is 68 years old and started whittling chains from single sticks of wood when he was 9. Number One is hanging on the wall of his living room. He figures he's made "a few" chains in that lifetime. Truth be told, there's no counting them.

Hundreds? I asked Ray. Well, sure. Maybe 1,200,... 1,400.

Not to forget hundreds more animal figures, whistles, doll furniture and other of what Ray called "these crazy things I manufacture."

He has but one good eye.

Dan Ward told me about Ray. Dan is the folk arts coordinator for the Cultural Resources Council of Syracuse and Onondaga County. He collects unusual, interesting folks like Ray. Dan told me he was so impressed with Ray's chain-whittling he brought him to the Onondaga Historical Association for an exhibit and demonstration.

It pleases Ray to show us what he can do. He got a kick out of coming back to Syracuse and being treated like the fine artist he is.

Especially, he said to me one day at Catfish Corners, if kids are involved. If there's one thing this man likes to do, it's work with kids. He couldn't get over what a good time he had whittling and talking about whittling at Lyncourt School a while ago.

"It does my heart good to be able to do something like that for kids," he said. "After I did that at Lyncourt, the kids sent me some cards. By God, that made me feel good!"

There was a time more people stopped by Ray's place than they do now. He had a "whittlin' house" next door to the trailer, which had to be turned into a residence to rent to help out one of his daughters. There was a sign by the road that said "*The Old Whittler. Museum of Fine Art. Raymond F. Dann.*"

The main room of that house was filled with wooden chains and other whittling of Ray's. His snapshots confirm that.

When he started renting it, the sign came down and

a lot of the master's work was taken to a daughter's house in another county.

Ray sold some of the things he made, especially the small animals and birds he did, but selling and pricing are problems for him. First, he may not want to give up a crazy invention of his. Second, how do you price a piece of work such as a chain when you've put hundreds of hours into it? I mean, Ray's got one wooden chain in that trailer with links so fine it took him a year to finish.

"Oh, I'll sell a smaller one," he explained. "But say I charge at least 15 cents an hour for my time, that's several hundred dollars for a chain."

Ray's not sure what started him whittling. His father, who was a quarryman, did a little, but nothing like the adventures his son got into over the years. Ninety-nine percent of what Ray knows he taught himself.

He's also not sure what started him into chains, except that as a kid he'd "whittle and whittle for hours with that little Remington jackknife of mine."

He rated the Remington "the best knife in the world," a basic tool for all whittling. Ray needed more particular blades as his work got more complicated, so he invented his own knives. He grinds the blades in a workshop out back and whittles the handles.

There is a distinction to be made here. Ray said he whittles with a jackknife. Equally fine artists carve, using a variety of tools, including power chisels and other high-tech processors. "If you use a power tool, you're not whittlin'," Ray told me with unfamiliar gruffness.

This whittler's preferred material is basswood. Pine is good too, although it's harder to cut. One time he did a chain from the pole of a roadside Burma Shave sign. Friends and neighbors save sticks for Ray. Others he cuts himself. Pieces are finished with sandpaper, but that's it. No glue, no varnish. "Just raw wood," according to the artist.

Ray whittles at the kitchen table, most of the time. Now and again, outside at his picnic table.

The kitchen has a hanging light and a 3-inch TV set. The single good eye doesn't appear to be a problem for Ray. That one eye, he said, sees everything.

Around the trailer, Ray prefers to dress easy. His favorite working outfit is a pair of old trousers and a shirt, open to the bellybutton.

Sometimes Ray will whittle every day, all day. Sometimes a week passes and he doesn't pick up a knife at all.

He invented a length of looped cotton string to hang from the lamp. That way he can suspend a stick on its way to being a chain and not have to worry about slamming it on the table and breaking it.

Ray begins a chain by scoring his stick with a pencil. The wood is notched where the whittler will form his links. Then he moves along, cleaning the wood out of each link as he goes.

Ray told me he enjoys a challenge. That's why he's developed all those tricky, fragile thing-a-ma-bobs among links of plain chain. Of course, even a hacker of wood will realize immediately that the ultimate challenge of building a chain from a single stick of wood is — you already guessed it — snapping the stick along the way.

When that happens, you just say you intended the chain to be that short, Ray said, with a wink of the good eye.

He swore he hadn't had a busted link or cage with a heart suspended in the middle in a year or more. "You take your time, you don't hurry," he explained.

I said to Ray I'd met only one other chain whittler. That was an old logger in the Adirondacks. I said it must take a certain skill, and a certain temperament to work at that scale. He agreed. Some folks have a knack for it, some don't. That doesn't mean you can't carve other things; chains could be beyond you, though.

"You need the right feel," according to Ray.

Now, Ray has these three women who have been coming in once a week for about a year. They asked him if he could teach them to whittle and he said, sure, why not? These are not the same women who swap coffee and kitchen tables with Ray by way of a little socialization at Catfish Corners. The old whittler will often bake a batch of muffins for such occasions.

He said to his pupils, watch me and do everything I do. He found one of the women was a flash and the others were middling, as far as working wood is concerned. The flash had the feel for the wood and the possibilities within each stick.

Ray has six children, three of them stepchildren from

his second wife's first marriage. That wife — Alice — died 2½ years ago and left a great hole in her husband's life. Alice, Ray believed, was "the greatest woman who ever lived."

Those hearts Ray likes to whittle into his chains are little mementos of the romance of Ray and Alice.

"You have to have love in this world," he said. "If you don't, you have nothing."

Each of Ray's chains is a bit more complicated than the last, judging from the samples I saw hanging next to the kitchen table.

For instance, we started talking about long chains, and Ray said he'd gone 7 feet and he's not sure how far he could go. He'd heard of a fellow in Japan who whittled one 40 feet.

Some day, he continued, "I'd like to make me a chain that would stretch all the way around the inside of the room here. But I'd never find a board that long."

This is another dream of Ray's:

"I'd have my nephew who cuts firewood bring me the biggest basswood log he can find. Three feet from the end of the log I'd cut a block as high as it was wide. I'd make it into a ball. Then I'd hollow out another ball inside of that. And I'd hollow that one, and another and another...

"I'd do that until I had 9 balls in that thing. The last one would be as small as that." He showed me the end of his thumb.

"I'd mount it on a display pedestal and put it out in the yard. Yep, one of these days I'm going to start that. And people will come by and ask me, 'Ray, how'd you do that?' " – *1988*

The Grandmother Tree

I stood between the awesome roots of a tree said to be the tallest in New York the other day. They call it "The Grandmother Tree."

It's quite a living thing. Quite a story goes with it.

I got to this antique of ours — it started growing about the time the Dutch turned over New York to the British — by driving to Charles L. Pack Demonstration Forest, which is north of the village of Warrensburg in Warren County. The 3,000-acre tract is a teaching base for our SUNY College of Environmental Science and Forestry.

The tree, an Eastern White Pine, grows in a virgin forest of 47 acres within the preserve. Two years ago it made the state's list of Famous and Historic Trees in New York.

According to the stats I got from the college, The Grandmother Tree is thought to be 315 years old. That means a seedling started to grow in 1674, when this part of New York was an even deeper wilderness than it is today.

It is 170 feet tall — I couldn't see the crown from where I stood — and 52 inches around. It rises at a slight angle from the floor of the forest these days.

The foresters estimated a while ago that Grandmother holds about 4,000 board feet of lumber, which is enough to build a small house, heaven forbid! The market value would be about $400.

In historical value, according to Don Ross, superintendent of the forest, “it is priceless.”

Charles Pack, a wealthy lumberman, donated the land to the college, along with a tract at Cranberry Lake, in 1927. Grandmother’s part of the forest was set aside as a “natural area in perpetuity” 30 years ago.

You reach it over a short nature trail.

The swamp land around the tract preserved the tree and its neighbors from logging in the 1830s. The Woodwards bought the land and started cutting trees for lumber in 1796. The tree stands today because one member of the family, Margaret S. Woodward, said no when her husband, John, wanted to take it down to buy a set of pewter dishes.

Margaret Woodward is the grandmother of The Grandmother Tree.

The story that came down to us from the Woodwards was that John had promised Margaret a set of dishes. Some say the set was pewter, some say silver. Money was hard to come by when this happened, in the depression days of the 1870s. John said he would raise the cash for the gift by cutting That Nice Tall White Pine Out Back.

The giant was accessible then, according to the story. The marshes had dried up.

Margaret would have no part of taking that grand tree for a set of dishes. She said she’d do without them, if need be. One tradition was that Margaret told John she’d chain herself to the pine to keep him from taking it with his ax.

John gave in, the story goes. Margaret didn't get her dishes just then, but she did take a place in history. And that shaft of bark and pulp took on a name.

When I talked to Kathryn Maltbie in Warrensburg about this, she said she wanted to set me straight about a couple of things. She is Margaret Woodward's great granddaughter.

"We never called it The Grandmother Tree," she said. "It was Grandmother's Tree, of course."

Another thing, my informant went on, "she did *not* chain herself to the tree to save it. That's ridiculous!"

Kathryn, who once had her picture taken standing in front of "Grandmother's Tree," said her own thought on the matter of silver vs. pewter dishes was that John surely would have wanted to buy his wife pewter, at that day and age. "They were poor people. I'm sure she wasn't interested in silverware."

Great Grandmother Woodward died in 1894 at the age of 88. The farm stayed in the family until Pack bought the land from five of her grandchildren in 1927.

Kathryn said kinspeople weren't unanimous about selling to the lumberman-turned-preservationist but she agreed with me "it was probably for the best, since the tree is protected."

"It really is quite a tale," she added.

Margaret and John's house still stands on the property, on the pond the Woodwards dug. Present day it is part of the complex that includes the office and a sawmill, where pine cut by the college in the forest is processed for sale to the public. Superintendent Don Ross and his family live in the Woodward homestead.

I had a peaceable walk of about 10 minutes from the parking lot next to the office to Margaret's tree. You get there by leaving Route 9, four miles north of Warrensburg.

The college provides trail maps and markers. In case you're ready to walk past it, The Grandmother Tree is marked by a small sign, stuck between the roots. It has a grandchild growing out of one of its flanks.

The only sounds I heard were the buzzing of the black flies in my ears and the planer back at the mill.

Later, Don Ross told me The Grandmother Tree is doing fine, thank you. Neither fire nor steel had touched this old-timer in more than three centuries, and if Don and the other foresters have their way, they never will. Lightning and wind, they have no control over.

"It's leaning a little, but it's in good shape," he explained. "The only threat might be a very violent wind storm." - *1989.*

Ray's Restaurant

Ray Fadden told me about the bear with one paw who used to read Ray's thoughts. A trap took the paw. After that, the burly king of the forest came to Ray's back yard — the landlord here calls his feed lot "Ray Fadden's Restaurant" — to eat the meat scraps Ray puts out for his friends.

Ray and his family live in the woods along County Route 30, in Franklin County north of Saranac Lake. The post office is Onchiota. Ray is a retired schoolteacher. He runs Six Nations Indian Museum, across the road from the house where he lives with his wife, Christine. His son, John, an artist who teaches in the Saranac school system, lives with his family a quarter-mile away.

The notion of a peaceable kingdom comes alive when you step out of the car at Onchiota.

Ray talked about his friend, the bear, as I followed him around the lot behind the house. Here, and around the museum buildings, are 135 feeding stations for the creatures who arrive flapping their wings or padding on all fours. My friend insists he owes it to them to provide them with extra food. This hobby costs Ray an arm and a leg — more than $1,000 a year for sunflower seed and cracked corn, by his estimate — but it must be done.

"I can't ignore my friends," Ray said to me.

Yes, the bear was his friend. He showed up at the back stoop one night and Ray knew what he'd come for. He has a butcher friend who provides bones and other scraps.

This feeding has been going on for years, so the Faddens have a modest bone yard out there beyond the porch that winds half way around the house.

Ray spread some seed out on the top of a tree stump for the birds, squirrels, chipmunks, skunks, porcupine, whatever. We heard ravens yelling at us from the trees. A large bird with the wing spread of an eagle took off from a crown nearby.

"They'll be licked clean by morning," Ray said. I picked a black fly out of my ear.

"You know," he went on, "it is possible to talk to animals. You can communicate, read each others' thoughts. I had a bear who came in here with a bad leg. It never healed. He let me pat him on the head. He licked my wrist. The last time I saw him I know he came to say goodbye. I let him go back to the earth."

The bear with one paw — Ray called him "Gimpy" — had a way of snorting his benefactor interpreted as a greeting. Ray would bow in return. Gimpy would bow back.

Bears are bolder than some of Ray's other friends, of course. They'll come right up to the door and knock, looking for food. Ray showed me the slashed window screens to document that. Sometimes a mother bear will send a cub to wake up the Faddens in the middle of the night.

Once Ray had a young boy visiting him who wanted

him to bring the "nice black dog" he'd found into the house.

"The dog was a bear cub," Ray said, chuckling. "I didn't think that was such a good idea."

They keep coming; Ray keeps feeding. A chipmunk rushed up to Ray, and he popped him a peanut. "I wonder what he's doing over here," he said after a minute of staring at his friend's twitching tail. "He belongs over on the other side of the road."

"Nobody feeds 'em like I do," Ray continued as we headed for the museum. "Ray Fadden's Restaurant, that's what this is. But what else can I do? They're starving."

Ray sees things going wrong in the Adirondacks, where the Faddens have lived nearly 30 years. Hungry creatures are part of the picture.

The flora is starving, as well, according to Ray. The pines aren't dropping the cones they used to. Acid rain, he believes, has weakened trees so that they snap when years ago they would have thrived.

Ray wouldn't have that many tree stumps around the house if it weren't for acid rain, he said.

"We're all having a hard time in the Adirondacks," Ray explained. "Either the developers want to cover the whole thing with cement or the acid rain will kill all of the fish and trees.

"Why, at the beginning of last winter, we got the worst storm I've ever seen. We had heavy snow, and it just snapped off the trees. Acid rain made them weak and they just broke off. I lost plenty of trees out back. You look around, and see those trees along the roads just slumped over."

My friend was getting fired up, the way he does. We got to the front door of the museum and it started to rain, of all things.

Ray worries about his own environment and everybody else's.

Foresters might argue with him about the trees. They don't think the chemicals in the precipitation that kill lakes in the Adirondacks has done equal damage to trees. If those trunks are curled over, or snapping off, the experts contend, it was the weight of the snow that did them in, not the poisons out of the Ohio smoke stacks.

Ray excused himself to go back to the house for pipe tobacco. Look around the building, he said. I did.

The Faddens built the museum themselves, and Ray either collected or made all of the exhibits, which is a considerable number. I'd been at Six Nations before, and each time I got dizzy, trying to take in everything. It's impossible to appreciate in one sitting.

When Ray quit teaching school — most of that among the Mohawks at Akwesasne — he and his wife, who is Mohawk, scouted out this spot near Buck Pond to teach Indian children about their own culture and show white people Indian ways and history.

Ray is just as emphatic about how Native Americans ought to be portrayed in history classes as he is about acid rain and feeding bears. He feels we have taught our children lies about the first settlers of the Americas.

The Fadden's museum is a small, Mom and Pop effort at putting the record right, by their measure.

Ray returned with a can of Union Leader tobacco. He sat in a chair he made from a deer hide. He lit his pipe and there was a knock at the door.

"Probably some Indians," Ray said. "They just keep coming. Won't let me do my work. Actually, I've turned this over to John. I'm just the janitor."

The visitors were a man and wife and their two daughters. They said they were from Korea. They didn't speak English well enough to explain to us how they had found their way to Onchiota.

All four headed for the sales counter, which Ray told me later should have been built at the back of the museum, not the front.

"Everybody wants to buy something," he said. Ray stocks a mix of cheap trinkets and fine crafts, including Mohawk baskets. The pamphlets and other printed materials, graced with drawings by Ray and John, who uses the Mohawk name "Kahionhes," are sold to buy "feed for my orphans."

"I had a woman out West who sent me money for seed," Ray said as one of the Koreans examined a rubber tom-tom. "But she died, unfortunately. I could use a few friends like that to help me out a bit with my seed money."

Ray asked the visitors if they'd like him to tell a story from one of the many story belts he made for the museum. I was relieved he didn't pick the longest piece of bead work in the world, which circles 75 feet of the museum. He grabbed a stick he uses as a pointer and moved it among the pictographs of a belt.

"One day an old man came into the village," he began.

The story concerned an ugly stranger who stopped at each of the clan huts and was turned away. Finally, a bear clan woman welcomed him into her house.

The Koreans were looking at the clocks on their wrists. "Have to go," the father said. Ray understood; they didn't know what on earth he was talking about.

"Thanks, grandpa," the man said.

"Sensai," I corrected. "Teacher."

Ray finished the story for me. In thanks, the ugly man showed the woman all of the herbs of the woodland and how to heal with them.

This inspired my host to try out his talk about the contributions of Native Americans on me. He mentioned baked beans, Irish potatoes, rubber, pop corn, peanuts, chewing gum, Egyptian cotton and democracy.

"That's why there's racism in America," Ray declared. "They don't teach the gifts of all of the cultures. Kids think everything came out of Europe. No wonder they think whites are superior. Truth is, every race has contributed."

Ray walked me to the car. I asked him if he had any wounded creatures he was nursing just then. No, he said; and no thanks to the "so-called hunters." He can't abide strangers who want to go into these woods and kill for no reason.

Nor the cruel sportsfolks who kill mothers and leave the babies to starve to death. Or the lousy shooters who wing a crow or an owl, then leave the bird to make its way; maybe to the Fadden place, maybe not.

Ray reminded me that Indians killed animals only when they were hungry. I remembered the Christmas card I got from Ray one year. It was decorated with pictures of the family's forest friends. In one corner, a Native American hunter was quoted, speaking to his quarry:

"*I am sorry that I had to kill you, little brother, but I had need of your meat. My children were hungry and crying for food. Forgive me, little brother. I honor your courage, your strength and your beauty.*"

No one of us is going to fix what needs fixing in the Adirondacks. That shouldn't keep us from honoring the courage, strength and beauty of a man who's trying. - *1989*

Bill Smith

Bill Smith gets paid to lie. He's going around and telling lies to people and singing in Onondaga County. I watched and listened to him the other day at Mundy Branch Library on Syracuse's West Side.

Bill's here from the town of Colton in St. Lawrence County. That's about three hours northeast of Syracuse, as the Adirondack ou-ah flies.

The Adirondack ou-ah is a bird with red, white and blue feathers, according to Bill. It lays five-sided eggs in the shape of stars.

This was one of the stories Bill told us at the library. He also told us about mosquitoes as big as wild turkeys.

One time, when Bill was a kid, he went out to the hog wallow and a legion of the super bugs came down from the hill and attacked him. He dived under a huge scalding kettle, but the critters bore right through it. Bill got away after he bent their beaks with a sledgehammer and the mosquitoes lifted the pot 30 feet in the air.

After that, we heard about Lanny Martin, who used a 12-gauge shotgun for a cane, and how Bill, who was one of 10 kids, took a bath regular as clockwork every Saturday night, whether he needed it or not. The Smiths drew but one bath in those days, our liar explained; each kid used the same water.

The best part came when Bill did the poem about Pierre LaBeau of Tupper Lake. Pierre used some leftover paint from the living room to do the seats in his outhouse. He got it at Frank Woolworth's first store up there in the North Country. The paint, which was pink, cost 10 cents a gallon. It didn't dry for weeks.

Bill said a very funny poem on the letter Pierre wrote to Frank Woolworth about that. And another funny poem by James Whitcomb Riley, also concerning outhouses.

That happened after Bill and his wife, Sal, who came to Syracuse with him, had supper with Dan Ward, the folklorist who works for the Cultural Resources Council. The council has a grant from the state Council on the Arts to let Bill carry Adirondack lore to us outlanders.

Bill is a Colton native. He's been a guide, trapper, logger, construction worker and teacher. The last eight years or so, he and Sal have been on the road telling lies and singing. Lately, he's brought out a cassette tape and a book of lies.

He also makes baskets from pounded black ash, although not as many as he used to. Wednesday, before supper, he showed us the whole nine yards of making baskets. It's a kind of science, according to Bill.

He got into the craft because of the Mohawks from Akwesasne who came to his father's logging camp. Dad had a huge ash swamp out back and an ash log is where you start to make an ash basket.

"I grew up watching people make baskets," Bill explained. "I grew up with an ax in my hand."

Bill stood in front of us in the library's assembly room. He had on a plaid felt shirt, logger's boots and pants held up by what our guest called "galluses." You might call them suspenders.

The table closest to Bill held his basket gear, including a sample splint log, the hide scraper he uses to peel bark from the splints, a homemade vice and a few sample baskets, which fairly sparkled. They looked so new and clean.

Bill lifted what he said was his "head ax" from the table to show us how a basket maker pounds a log to loosen the pulp and to peel back the growth rings. This is a very delicate and critical step.

"People want to make baskets but if they can't pound a log right, they ruin it," he explained. "You have to get a rhythm going." He swung the ax once without striking the log and made a noise with his mouth.

"You give it a good, solid rap so it hurts your ears. But the only way you know is to find it yourself. It's hard to get young fellows who know how to pound an ax."

Bill's favorite basket is the model he's used himself in the woods since he was a kid. That's the pack basket, which some people insist was invented by Indians in New York state. Bill said he believed that. Likely it was the Algonquians.

When I asked him, Bill said he once had a lighter, newfangled fabric and aluminum pack but he gave it away and went back to his basket. He just liked it better; it didn't snag on limbs and spill the pack on you.

In fact, he said, it was possible to kill a deer in the

woods, field dress it and stow all of the usable parts in his pack, which is made Algonquin-style, in the shape of a great splint bottle.

Bill seems to like baskets. Likes them a lot. He pointed to a new pack.

"This is a breathing thing," he said. "Even though you cut down the tree, the wood isn't dead. It breathes moisture from the air." - *1990*

Northville

Paul Decker took me to see the chimney swifts return to Northville Sunday night. It was quite a sight.

Paul's the Fulton County coroner. He's into his 10th year in the job. The birds? Well, they've been coming into the northeast corner of Paul's territory for years. Fifty, maybe. Maybe longer.

We're told they fly into the Adirondack Mountain Park from the headwaters of the Amazon River. Northville sits on an arm of Great Sacandaga Lake, north of Gloversville.

No one seemed to have kept books on the event. The only thing you'd get agreement on in this village is that these crazy little birds — they are smaller than a house sparrow — arrive every year on the same day, May 6.

There's more.

Not only it is the same day, which happened to be the birthday of a local worthy, but they also roost in the same chimney that's been their summer home at least 50 years.

Each May 6, as dusk settles on the mountains, the swifts funnel into the smoke stack of Frank Hubbell's old linoleum rug fastener factory.

"Like smoke in reverse," Dr. Richard Fisher of Ithaca had said to me.

That's exactly the way it was Sunday night.

"Homecoming," according to Terry Warner, the town historian.

Hundreds of birds came home to Frank Hubbell's chimney while hundreds of people stood around watching. That included me and the coroner and a TV cameraman from Schenectady.

Across Bridge Street, Terry Warner sold history books and postcards on the porch of the old Mosher feed store. Across North Second Street, they were selling popcorn and chimney swift T-shirts in front of the Adirondack Sportsman store.

The high school band didn't play this year, as was its habit. Something about it being Sunday night. Likewise, the speeches by the mayor and folks from Rotary were scratched.

According to Terry, some villagers thought the music spooked the birds. They surely were spooked a couple of years ago when a TV crew poured artificial light onto the stack. The birds refused to claim their roosts until the lights were shut off.

Swifts started to flock in numbers about 7:30 p.m. Sunday.

So did spectators. Several had long lens and tripods on their cameras. All of the lens pointed toward what Northville calls "The Hubbell Chimney," which is 80 feet tall and surrounded by a chain-link fence. The rest of the factory is long-gone.

The birds flocked, dispersed, moved around the

block and flocked again. Several times.

At 8:03 p.m., one of them popped into the stack.

The rest followed.

Yes, quickly, two by two. Then three by three, four by four.

As into a funnel. As smoke, pulled backward.

A minute later, only three birds remained aloft. Then a pair dived into The Hubbell Chimney.

We clapped. Someone shouted, "All right!"

Then, the last little fellow went in.

We applauded and cheered.

After that, we went home.

Paul Decker wanted me to see the swifts — it was his first May 6 at Northville, too — as part of a quick tour of Fulton County by pale moonlight. He'd promised me that when we met a month ago. The coroner grew up nearby at Caroga Lake.

The birds repeat their ritual almost every night in the village until about Aug. 20, when they start flying south again. "And in the morning, between 5 and 6, they come out of the chimney the same way," Terry Warner explained. "It never ceases to amaze me."

Terry said the chimney went up with Frank Hubbell's factory in 1891. It remained when the place burned, about 1927. One villager told me May 6 was Hubbell's birthday. Terry said it was the birthday of Walker LaRowe, who sold appliances in the old feed store. Walker was the person who first noticed the precision of the swifts' return and institutionalized it "maybe 50 years ago."

There's more than spectacle at work here. Northville loves its swifts because they're great bug-eaters.

"They leave the chimney and spread out into the Sacandaga Valley and eat mosquitoes," Terry explained. "Each one eats about 1,500 a day."

Later, I talked by phone to Richard Fisher, an ornithologist, retired from Cornell University. His State Museum bulletin, "The Breeding Biology of the Chimney Swift," is the basic book here.

He's never been to Northville but was cheered up by my report.

The swifts, according to this expert, are regular in their migration and probably are in Northville, and other locations, before they circle the chimney. He'd seen a few in Ithaca last week and had been told a large flock flew into the Sherman Elementary School chimney there Monday at dusk.

An unknown signal sends the birds into a chimney as a flock, Dr. Fisher said. He doesn't know what it is. "Some kind of extra-sensory perception," he explained. - *1990*

Mike's Cabin

Mike Virkler and I took the main haul into Watson East Triangle of Herkimer County a couple of weeks ago. Mike at the wheel of his four-wheel drive Sierra with a chaw of tobacco in his cheek and a monologue about The Adirondacks and conservationism on his lips.

He wanted me to see his camp at Buck Lake. He's not sure how long it's going to be there.

Mike's 85. He started coming to this remote logging tract north of Lowville 63 years ago. He's hunted it, fished it, guided it and admired it ever since.

Just now he owns a quandary that's one acre of the bigger picture of The Adirondacks. The camp Mike and his wife, Hilda, put on a bluff at Buck Lake 29 years ago is at the edge of the argument between New Yorkers who want to preserve our great wilderness and those who want to use it.

The Virklers live in Castorland, that's 32 miles and 2½ hours of mostly logging road from Buck Lake. Mike walked into Watson East to hunt as a young man. Then he joined a hunt club in the triangle. A dozen years later, in the early 1960s, he left the club and built the cabin of his dreams on an acre of land he rented from International Paper Co., which had cut timber in these woods since the 1880s.

Mike said he figured the lot would be his as long as he paid the rent. He didn't figure on taxes going up and logging going out.

Five years ago, the company sold 16,700 acres of Watson East to the state, to add to the forest preserve. At the time, its real estate division told the Watson East club members the tract had to be sold as a single piece and a buyer couldn't be found.

The hunting camps — there are 11 besides Mike's Buck Lake Club — could stay until Sept. 10, 1991. After that, the area's part of the Oswegatchie Great Forest preserve.

State law on forest preserves is followed here. The tenants have to "*restore the land to a condition satisfactory to*" International Paper and the state. That condition, under the company's sale agreement, means removal of man-made structures from the tract.

Including the one made by this man, Mike Virkler.

Most of the clubs in the triangle plan to close their camps and walk away. "Let the state burn 'em," Jim Duflo of Kelly Hills Club said to me last week.

Mike has an offer from the Department of Environmental Conservation which might preserve the place. Last week, he said he thinks the offer's too late.

Mike started us toward the camp with a drive through his tree farm, 191 acres developed by Mike and his father since 1916. He's still cutting pines in the plantation, although not by himself, the way he used to. He also ran a coal and fuel oil business in Castorland for 30 years.

There have been Virklers in this part of Lewis County since the 1830s. Mike drove and talked about them as we ate the egg and olive sandwiches Hilda packed us. He didn't bother to hide the fact he's proud of his roots, the ones in his family and in his woodlands.

He pointed out the way his roadways run straight among the lines of trees. How the wildflowers and game coexist with his crop. How straight and tall some of those pines grow.

"I wanted you to see this in contrast to what we'll see later in the forest preserve," he explained.

Mike said he hoped I wouldn't pin a quick label to him. If I had to, what would it be?

"How about conservationist," he replied, "someone who believes in the wise use of natural resources. I never called myself an environmentalist. That's a fashionable, misused word. I call those people the 'environmental evangelists.' They're public relations people with millions of dollars to spend."

Mike, I guessed, is an independent Yankee from New York who wants to live without evangelism and government touching his life.

We stopped at Croghan Meat Market for sausage and a roll of the famous bologna sausage that's made there. Outside of the hamlet of Belfort, Mike mentioned that the Yanceys — pronounced "Yoncey" — are Hilda's family. They helped him build the cabin.

We talked about glacial rocks, sugar bushes and

eskers, the sand ridges snaking through the Adirondack mountains. The Virklers' camp sits on an esker. When I noticed my host's knowledge of geology, I got him to admit he'd studied the subject in college, along with Romance languages and German.

Mike is Class of 1923, Hamilton College.

He put his German to use as an Army officer in World War II for six years. He was assigned to German POW camps in the United States. He also studied at Heidelberg during a tour of Europe after college and at McGill, in Canada.

"Outside of that," Mike said, lighting his corncob pipe, "I'm more or less illiterate."

The terrain under the Sierra got steeper, narrower and guttier as we closed in on the camp. We traveled the main haul, the trail cut for loggers with horses 100 years ago. Between 1927 and 1986, Mike and his brother-in-law, Joe Yancey, guided hunters in with a team of horses hauling a wagon.

When we passed into Herkimer County, he announced: "This is the wilderness, by bureaucratic decree. The state buys it, and it becomes wilderness. They take the best and leave the rest."

The man knows the woods. Mike's like a topographic map that talks and tells stories about the ponds, forks in the road and landings where the lumbermen piled their logs.

We passed a landing where Wendell Still had the last logging camp. I noticed piles of rotting timber, a rusty snow-plow and the hollow frame of a cabin.

"Some of this is worse than the Belleau Woods I saw when I was in Europe after World War I," he said. Mike doesn't think the state is a worthy caretaker of the wildernesses it buys. He thinks it's foolish to covet more.

I'd heard the same sentiment when I talked about Watson East with Jim Duflo, another of the old-time hunting campers. Jim sells real estate in Lowville and knows the wilderness marketplace.

"It's a pity the state has to do what they do," Jim said. "It's because of the do-gooders in the Sierra and Audubon clubs. What they try to do is admirable, but it's at someone else's expense. The state owns 3 million acres now, and they can't take care of it."

Jim explained how International Paper at first tried to sell all of the 16,000 acres in the triangle to the hunt clubs at a high price, then in parcels of a few thousands acres, which still weren't affordable.

The company formed a real estate division and cut a deal with the state for the land in 1986.

"We had no choice, take the lease or leave it," Mike recalled. "It was a ripoff by the paper company with the approval of DEC. In a way, I blame the governor for pushing the purchase of the triangle. He's only hearing what the loudmouth environmental evangelists say to him, and he thinks that's the thing to do. I'd like to bring him up here for the night."

One of the sights Mike would point out to Mario Cuomo would be piles of tree cuttings along the road, which are marked with pink flags since DEC took over as forest manager. In the old days, such brush would be left to return to nature in the woods; now it's supposed to be hauled out, so not to disfigure the wilderness.

We passed a pink blaze, and Mike said to me, "Nice spot for a condo, don't you think? I'm sure some developer will want to put one up here. Sure. There's no scenery to speak of, and the fishing's no good any more."

Mike continued, "Fish pirates ruined it. They take out fish for an entire year during the first week of fishing. I volunteered to manage Buck Lake to bring back the trout, but the DEC wouldn't let me.

"And the road-running poachers are killing the deer all season with impunity. The game protector up here retired, and they didn't replace him."

We watched a young buck cross in front of us.

"You know, I compare the state buying the triangle to communism. They're eliminating private enterprise and initiative. They're taking the camps away from people who've been paying their way over the years and turning it over to the public, the proletariat, for free. With about the same results we've seen with communism."

I said to Mike somebody's going to think you hunters just want to have the wilderness to yourselves. He shook his head.

"They've got all the playground they need for the recreationists. You know the public has trashed a lot of the wilderness by overuse. And as a youth, I did a lot of climbing myself. I think the DEC is trying to steer them over here, but they're not interested."

When we got to the trail head into camp, Mike spotted truck tracks in the dirt. The puddles were muddy. Someone's in there. He's sensitive to visitors because vandalism has increased at the camps in the last five years. That's one reason Mike strapped on a gun belt with his .357 Magnum before we left Castorland.

No trouble today, though. The visitor was a welcome one, the mayor of Castorland.

The mayor's Mike's pal, Rich Widrick. Rich worked on the camp. They pitched tents on the bluff during the two summers it took them to finish the main building and woodshed.

Rich had a fire in the big stone fireplace Mike put up using some of his geologic wonders. Smoke curled from the chimney. There was a fire in the stove, too. Rich is camp cook; he had venison bourguignon stewing in a black frying pan.

We smiled and went inside Mike's cabin. We were wet from the rain and tired from the trip to 1,800-foot elevation and the headwaters of the West Branch of the Oswegatchie River.

The cabin's one big room with windows to the pond, which the Virklers renamed a lake "because it doesn't sound so slimy," according to Mike. The log walls are tongue-and-groove construction. Mike and his helpers cut them with chain saws and made them snug without using chink.

The roof's of quartersawn white-pine shingles. Not a nail in there, nor anywhere else; gravity and pegs do the trick.

Mike and Hilda's place is a wonder of convenience and built-ins. There's even a homemade mouse trap under the sink. A tin can is stretched over a pail of water on a string. The can is coated with peanut butter.

Rich, Mike and I sat at the table and feasted on Rich's stew and potatoes and a salad Mike mixed as we talked. All the ingredients but the lettuce are stowed on a shelf under the table, which was built by Mike from a 250-year-old windblown hard maple. Some of the spices were in the burl bowls Mike carves in the winter at home.

It was quiet, real quiet, except for wind shivering the bear fence on the outside walls. Dark, too.

"There ain't nothing out there but what's out there," Rich said solemnly.

I didn't need to ask my companions why they like Buck Lake so much. But I did anyway.

"I come here to relax," Mike said.

Rich nodded.

We poured coffee from the pot steaming on the stove. Mike sat so the flames in the grate lighted him from behind. He looked down at some notes he'd made and then he told me about what the DEC visitors proposed when they visited the cabin the week before.

Later I heard the ideas from one of the visitors, Tom Brown of Watertown, DEC administrator for the region.

"We think this is a really exceptional piece of skilled

carpentry and craftsmanship," Tom explained. "The purpose of our meeting with Mike was to discuss some more practical uses of the camp. We wanted to find out what he wanted to do."

No, he said. Thing is DEC had no intention of destroying it Sept. 10.

A classification process will take about two years after the state has title. This involves recommendations by the Adirondack Park Agency and DEC to the governor as to whether Watson East is to be "wild forest" or "wilderness."

If it is to be wild forest, Tom said the cabin might be preserved, possibly as a shelter for hikers and campers or an interim ranger station. If it's a wilderness it's to be, without a trace of Mike or any other man, then Tom would like to explore the idea of moving the camp to the Adirondack Museum at Blue Mountain Lake.

That night at Buck Lake Mike told me he appreciated Tom's consideration "even though it wasn't possible to come up with anything acceptable to us, or them, I guess."

He said he didn't think the cabin can be moved, because of its construction. He also didn't like the notion, offered by Tom, of staying on after the 10th as a caretaker. Independent woodsman that he is, they're not going to put Mike Virkler on any state payroll.

The main thing, though, was that he didn't think the cabin's going to be there very long after he and Hilda pack the truck and move down the road for the last time.

"It's a toss-up," Mike said, "who will trash it first, the

vandals or the bears."

The next morning we woke up to the smell of Rich's eggs, coffee and johnnycake corn bread. I walked around in the mists taking pictures, and Mike washed in a bowl heated on the stove. Then he fed the three Canada jays who eat out of his hand from the front porch.

I called Mike the next week to see if he'd decided.

"We had another break-in at the camp the week after you were up there," he said. "They took some handicrafts and antiques and deflated the tires on the ATV and tote wagon. They stole my rain gauge. That ends 26 years of keeping records for the DEC and Geological Survey."

Mike sounded as if he wanted to cry.

"I think that's proof New York state already has more than it can handle. If the cabin's still there after the 10th, those people are going to burn it. They want what we've built up. And if I'm there, they're afraid they'll be reported for doing something illegal."

When I asked, Mike said he thought he knew his enemies. He thinks they resent him because of how he's reported their illegal activities in Watson East. So, he and Hilda took most of their belongings with them to Castorland when they broke camp last Sunday.

Had he made this decision, then?

"I feel there's no decision to make," Mike replied. "I'm being realistic." - *1991*

FOOTNOTE: In 1992, the Virklers' cabin was taken apart and moved to the Adirondack Museum, where crews reassembled it as an exhibit. "Better than burning it," Mike said.

Our Lone Prairie

Maybe we didn't know, but we have a prairie in New York state. I didn't, until a couple of years ago.

It's about 15 miles northwest of Watertown near Chaumont, in Jefferson County.

Very back country. Very rare. Very delicate.

A while ago, I saw ruts in the turf of this prairie of ours made by a logging crew five years ago. They're likely to be there 40, 50 years down the road.

Experts gave the prairie a name in 1984: Chaumont Barrens. One of them, Dr. Robert Zaremba of The Nature Conservancy, said it's "one of the most exciting botanical sites in the Northeast."

The barrens started to develop after the retreat of the last glacier. No one is sure why it never developed any more than it did.

Folks thereabouts didn't give the area much notice, except to wonder how they could do much more than graze cattle and cut timber on glacial till less than a foot to bedrock.

They called the place Burnt Rock.

Why, the soil cover's so thin, in the summer the limestone underneath heats up and the grasses turn brown and burned long before the first frost.

There is one thing you'd notice, if you were a neighbor to this spread of burnt rock. That's the downy, pink plumes of the flowers growing by the thousands in the meadows over yonder.

A field of the flowers gone to seed in early June is enough to remind you there are still wonders left to be seen in this world, even northwest of Watertown.

That plant's the prairie flower. For years, botanists thought it had left New York state.

Gerry Smith showed me a meadow of it last month.

Gerry is a land steward for The Nature Conservancy. He toured a small troop of members through Chaumont Barrens in early June. I went along.

A couple of summers ago I'd taken a back road near Depauville. I wanted to see the "buffalo grass" I'd heard about. I stopped at Bill Blance's place.

Bill showed me the grass and joked about raising buffalo on his spread. He said he might open up a hot dog stand because of all the strangers who kept dropping by.

I'd missed the wonder of prairie smoke gone to seed. Come back another time, Bill suggested. "It's the prettiest little flower I've ever seen."

When I did return, it was in the charge of Gerry Smith, a bird watcher who looks over the barrens and other properties of the conservancy in this part of upper New York. The last time we talked was at another protected site, El Dorado Beach on Lake Ontario.

We parked along a dirt road in the Town of Lyme.

On the way in Gerry told us we were walking into one of the organization's largest holdings. The Central New York Chapter has title to 834 acres of barrens and is raising money to purchase about 700 more.

The literature I read ahead of time called Chaumont *"a calcareous pavement complex that is a prime example of an extremely rare prairie community."*

"This is the jewel in the crown of the conservancy for the Northeast," Gerry said as we passed a patch of yellow rock harlequin. "There aren't that many spots like this on the entire planet."

The conservancy in New York has 49,000 members. The mission is to "*preserve plants, animals and natural communities that represent the diversity of life on Earth by protecting the lands and waters they need to survive.*"

This is carried out in cooperation with the state's Natural Heritage Program. As soon as rarities such as Chaumont are identified, the conservators move in and try to buy it.

This happened at the barrens in 1984 after Carol Reschke, community ecologist for the heritage program, discovered Chaumont. The conservancy had just bought Limestone Cedars Preserve nearby. Carol looked at its neighborhood on aerial photographs and then in person.

"*At first,*" she wrote in the conservancy newsletter, "*these communities look like barren, rocky landscapes with only an occasional tree or scrub.*" However, a closer look showed her an undisturbed area of diverse plants and animals, including several rare species.

The barrens were home to a bird called the Prairie Warbler. Also such rare plants as Michigan lily, prairie dropseed, white cammass, rams-head slipper, Crawe's sledge, scarlet Indian paintbrush, early buttercup and needle-leaf starwort.

Carol said she really knew she was onto something when she found the meadows of prairie smoke, an old friend from the dry prairies of southern Wisconsin.

She knew, too, that the most recent record of the plant was in 1842, when the state botanist, John Torrey, reported prairie smoke had been collected on rocks in Watertown. When the state plant people searched again in 1981, they couldn't find it.

They listed the plant as "extirpated." Gone.

Later, Carol and her helpers discovered the Olympia marble on the barrens. That's a rare butterfly. Also a kind of moss only known in New York from fossils.

As we crunched along — being as gentle of foot as we could — Gerry explained that his organization has a PhD student at work on the interesting question of why this area remained the botanic time capsule it did after the ice melted thousands of years ago.

Most natural areas become wooded over time, Gerry said. Why not Chaumont? Was there a natural disturbance to keep out the woody plants and allow the grass and wildflowers to dominate?

Was it fire? Or regular flooding in the spring, and drought in late summer?

Fragile, for sure, Gerry said, pointing to the old loggers' ruts in the prairie where trees had been pulled out as recently as five years ago.

We stepped a bit lighter through the pink meadow. Smoke plants brushed our knees as we passed.

"Someday," Gerry was saying, "we hope to understand why this is so special." - *1991*

Dudley Frasure

Dudley Frasure's gone. A master passes.

Dud died two weeks ago at Maplehurst Farm, Chenango County, where he was born, 80 years ago Sept. 1. He was working on his papers at the time.

My friend did many things, most of them very well. He'll be remembered as the inventor of the Frasure Adirondack Pack Basket.

He also was a naturalist, writer, calligrapher, artist, photographer, philosopher and weaver of splints and Christmas wreaths. Not to forget a fine pal to many of us.

Dorothy Marsters, his companion of many years, tells me Dud had been OK. He'd had a bad spell with his heart two years ago; it put him in the hospital, a place he very much did not want to be.

It seemed that vital organ in Dud's chest worked too hard. They gave him something to slow it down and sent him home.

I didn't think it odd that Dud's heart ran faster than most of ours. His head did, too.

"He was upstairs working on his art and his writing," Dorothy explained. A sudden heart attack took him. We agreed that was the way he'd wanted it. Dud wasn't one to wind down his days in a hospital bed, with tubes stuck into him.

I remembered a letter he wrote to me in that rolling calligrapher's pen of his when my mother died a few years ago. I fished it out of a fat file folder I have of letters and fliers and clippings from Maplehurst.

"*My mother died New Year's Eve 1961,*" Dud wrote, "*and I yet mourn her passing. She died quickly and quietly at 79, lying on the couch.*

"*Her last words were, 'Dudley, turn out the lights on the Christmas tree.' And she was gone. She was active to her last breath. ... I grew out of a childhood fast the night (8:45 p.m.) she passed away.*"

I first made it to Dud's old yellow farmhouse in the valley south of Sherburne village a dozen years ago. I'd been told there wasn't a finer practitioner of the craft of making an Adirondack pack basket than Dudley H. Frasure. Dave Goff, the craft wizard of Oneida, put me on to that.

The tradition is that Native Americans made our first pack baskets. Dud simply picked up on the tradition and improved it.

The roots of this strong, modest carrier are gnarled and distant; some people who seem to know what they're talking about insist the original of Dud's handiwork was native to the Adirondacks, or close by.

I have a copy of the leaflet Roland Miller wrote for state Conservation Department in 1948 which staked a claim for the Abenaki Indians as originators of the Adirondack pack basket.

Roland had interviewed an Abenaki chief, Julius Paul

Dennis of Old Forge, about this: *"(Dennis) says that it was on his reservation (just over the New York border in Quebec) that the basket was designed and made to replace the old Canadian tumpline pack.*

"Chief Dennis, with the modesty characteristic of his peaceloving and industrious tribe, has high praise for the skill of the early whites who also wove the basket, but he says they copied the art from his people."

Years after that was written I had the good luck to meet the chief's son, Maurice, at Old Forge. Maurice told me he'd made his first pack from the wood of a black ash tree when he was 15. He weaved them, off and on, until he died.

Maurice and Dud and many other naturalists I've met hated those soft packs hikers use today. They wanted a sturdy presence at their backs, with plenty of room for the gear someone needs in the woods.

Dud always smiled when people mentioned he ought to be living in the Adirondacks if he made Adirondack pack baskets.

We'd once explored the idea of an article about him in a regional magazine called Adirondack Life. The editor turned out to be a diehard regionalist.

He'd be interested, he wrote me, "*if he lived in the Adirondacks.*"

We didn't see the point. What's the difference where you are if your heart's into your work?

Dud's heart was into his work.

He once said to me he'd never worked for anyone:

"I've got my health, and I certainly wouldn't trade anything for retirement. I've never been more alive. It's always a challenge. You know, there are no two trees or batch of splints alike.

"No, I've never had a monotonous day in my life."

Dud had worked his father's farm, but allergies to cattle and hay dust got to him. He left the valley in 1945 and moved up the hill to Hunt's Mountain, where he and his friends built a cabin. They called the place "Camp Comfert."

Comfert came to have great meaning for Dud. He stayed on the oversized hill five years and found himself. He also experimented with weaving splints, with the help of his pal Charlie Prenis from South Hamilton, and a couple of experienced weavers named Bill Houck and Ed Webb. Dud said Ed was "part Indian."

That first basket was a terrible-looking thing, according to its maker.

Afterward, well, Dud took the traditional ways of pounding splints from an ash log and added his own adaptations. One of those was an invention standing today in Dud's basement: the "Frasure Monstrosity."

This is a ferocious machine Dud put together from drag saw parts, gears, belts, a motor, an anvil. He did it to duplicate the movement of the human arm.

When he came home to the valley from the mountain, Dud decided he had to have something to pound ash logs into splints. Otherwise, he said he'd spend his time doing that and couldn't concentrate on producing packs of quality in quantity.

He made more than 5,000 in 40 years. Lately, he couldn't keep up with the orders and would take time out to catch a breath and work on his journal.

You see, he wrote to me once, *"I'm making these baskets for just one reason: So I can eat and make a partial living; no other reason."*

A practical man, sure, but an artist also.

I've been going through all the little fliers and pamphlets Dud composed and illustrated for his clients and friends. In one, "*Our Policy 1985,*" he wrote:

"Our craft is old and slow, one step at a time and 50 years behind the times, but it is honest. We sleep well.

"There is much satisfaction in making something well, all by hand; and we shall continue making the same, strong, old-fashioned Adirondack pack basket that has established such a good name for us since 1946.

"You can buy this basket and get service if you need it. You know who made it."

Then Dud, as was his habit, added a quote from John Ruskin, a favorite writer. *Quality's never an accident,* Ruskin said.

Dud left a dozen or so unfinished packs in his shop. He talked about getting back and finishing them, but he never did. He told Dave Goff the task seemed too imposing, after he'd been out of it a while.

Maybe Tim Wimmer will complete the master's work some day. Tim, who lives in Canastota, apprenticed with Dud at Sherburne in 1984 after the state Council on the Arts gave him a grant to teach another basketmaker how to create a Frasure.

Tim's a graduate of the state College of Environmental Science and Forestry in Syracuse. He met Dud in 1983 after he and a friend tried to do a pack on their own. Dud shared all 52 steps with Tim, and let Tim copy his patterns. Tim knows how Dud rigged his straps too; this is vital to the basket's uniqueness.

Tim told me the other day he hasn't made a basket in four years. He will, though, as soon as he finishes the house he's building. This is important to him, he said, now that the torch's been passed. He hopes The Monstrosity will be passed, too.

Tradition survives. Sleep well, Dud. - *1992*

A "River Rat"

If you're at the decoy show in Clayton, Jefferson County, you may get a chance to meet a community treasure who says he's one of the last of the old-time river rats.

His name is Capt. Bill Massey. He's 77 and lives at Massey Point, on a bay of the St. Lawrence River at Waddington, St. Lawrence County.

Understand, it's like being presented a badge of honor to be a "river rat."

Bill shook his head when I asked if he minded if I called him that. "A librarian up here once asked me what a river rat was," he replied. "I said, 'You're lookin' at one.'

"I've run the river most of my life. I know the St. Lawrence, from Massena, out to the lake, better than any man alive."

He's also the last of the region's traditional carvers of pine blocks into the figures of ducks that look so real, to the ducks, they swoop to the water to be killed by a hunter's gun. This was a grand tradition of the river; it began to die as a practical craft when Bill reached middle age.

Bill's the third generation of Masseys who ran the river, shot ducks and carved decoys, which he pronounces DE-coys.

Add to the roll call Bill's credentials as storyteller,

boatman, mechanic, historian, fiddler and artist in several forms and woods and you'll see why I needed to make two trips to Waddington, last fall and this spring, to take the man's measure.

Besides, I wanted to meet a fellow Yorker who's been nominated, by the non-profit Traditional Arts in Upstate New York Foundation, for a national Heritage Fellowship. These actual badges of honor — 15 are given each year through the Smithsonian Institution — are our equals to Japan's "living treasures" awards.

Bill's town, where he and his wife, Vera, have lived since 1968, is halfway between The Burg, Ogdensburg, and Massena, in St. Lawrence County.

Vera's from New York City. They met during the years Bill piloted ferry boats in and around the Atlantic and its Hudson River harbors.

Bill? Well, he's as ratty a river person as they come. His mother Maggie bore him in a tent on an island called Indian Camp toward the Canadian side of the river.

The Masseys were loyalists in Canada way back. There's a village near Toronto by that name, in fact.

His grandfather, also Bill, came onto the St. Lawrence by way of Canada's Grenadier Island, down river from Rockport. Old Bill had 13 brothers; 11 of them drowned in the river or Lake Ontario.

Such are hazards of taking to the water to make a living. You live by it; you die by it.

"They were all captains on lake schooners," Bill

explained to his astonished visitor from inland.

Great Uncle Len Massey survived to be crowned, several times, "King of the Lakes." Bill said a man earned that title up to The Burg by outlasting opponents in bare-fisted boxing matches that went on for hours.

Bill has Uncle Len's fiddle.

"He told me he'd give me the fiddle if I learned to play a tune," Bill explained. "I learned 'Pop Goes the Weasel' and got the fiddle. I made my money when I was a kid fiddlin' and trappin'. I fiddled up around Hammond. There were four of us, all friends. We'd play 'til daylight for 25 cents."

Bill's full of stories. "Being on the river most of my life," he said, "I've got a lot of nice little stories, and they're the truth."

Sometimes he gets together with Bill Smith, an Adirondack treasure, and they play off river and mountain yarns.

During a pause of a few seconds in our talks, Bill would look at me with a twinkle in his eye and ask, "Did I tell you about? ..." That's one reason it took me several hours and two stops to get Bill onto paper.

The other day, for instance — it was cool on the river and smoke curled from the stack in Bill's shop — we started with a cup of coffee with Vera in the living room and ended up in the shop, down at the end of the yard, with a stopover above the garage, where the Masseys stow their decoys and other curiosities and memorabilia.

We sat at the end of the main room of Vera and Bill's

log house, which has a picture window to the bay. The room's floor to ceiling with Bill's interests, from ducks he's carved, to racks of his muzzle-loader guns, to paintings, to hunting trophy heads and other souvenirs of what Bill will admit has been a good, interesting life.

Those canes over there? He carved them from burled branches of pines he picked up in Florida, where he used to hunt snakes. Bill said he let the odd shapes of the wood tell him what to carve.

He also makes knife handles and decorates powder horns, too.

Yes, that's the hide of one of his Florida kills, 8 feet, 3 inches of snake skin stretched against the wall. He got the 14-point buck hunting in Canada in 1949.

Bill wanted me to know while he's handy with guns, Vera is too. The Masseys trap-shot together for years; trophies on the walls prove that. Bill only outshot Vera once, according to him.

If you want talk deadeyes, Bill will remind you that his dad, Capt. "Bob" Massey, may have been one of the most accurate and fastest shooters of game birds ever on the flyway. Bill doesn't hold back when he talks about his father, who died in 1950.

"He was the most knowledgeable man on the St. Lawrence River," Bill said.

Period.

You'd have a hard time thinking up a character as fascinating as Bob Massey, from what I've been able to learn.

Bob followed his father as head boatman at the Ice Island Shooting Club. He also was a guide. He hunted and fished for the market, built and raced boats and carved decoys, while he captained one of those lake schooners.

Bill has a picture of his father on a wall of his shop. It shows Bob in 1930, in a duck blind on Ice Island, ready to pump a few hundred rounds. The photograph captured Bob's hearty frame — his son says he was built like a fullback — and a face that can't hide the fact Bob's mother, Emma Massey, was a member of the Mohawk Nation.

All three of the Masseys who lived on the river — Bill, Bob and Grandpa Bill — carved ducks for hunting. Bill will show you his three prize decoys, one each by three generations, 1860, 1898 and 1932. The craft perfected its way to Bill; his work seems to be the most serious in the family.

Bill admitted his father's work was sloppy. But then the idea in the heyday of market shooting was to kill as many ducks as you could in the shortest time and get the carcasses on the train at Hammond for the rich people in New York City. The lures needed only to pull the birds out of the sky, not look pretty.

"My father told Vera once that a good decoy was a 2-by-8 with a potato stuck on a nail," Bill said. "One time he saw me putting eyes into my heads. He laughed. Whatya needs eyes for? By the time the ducks can see the eyes in the decoy, it's too late."

Bill paused and looked at some of his own birds on the back shelf of the shop.

"But it's nice to see a nicely painted duck."

Thousands of decoys were carved, mostly in the winter, for shooting on the St. Lawrence. Early on, you wanted a carving that looked something like a bird, stayed upright most of the time and endured over the seasons. A nicely painted and shaped duck came later among the mass-producers.

Bill figures he's a literal bridge from the era of his grandfather and father — market hunting of migratory birds was outlawed by the federal government in 1918 — and modern carvers, some of whom, he says, never hunted a duck.

"There's a lot of carvers better than I am," Bill remarked as we sat in folding chairs in his shop. "I carried the tradition, from old-time ducks in the '30s til the '50s, when the new fellers took over. I'm the last one. I never thought I'd be the last one."

Bill's birds start with white pine blocks, sawed from clean logs from the mill. He dries his wood at home. The only mechanical device involved in the process is a band saw, which he uses to rough out heads and bodies.

He carves the head first, then puts it aside until the body's finished. Three coats of paint are needed.

He uses two small knives, a Stanley rasp and five small chisels. Bill kills a week on a bird, on the average.

Each is made individually, on the master's whim. Most are carved to float in the water, even though Bill knows many of his birds end up on our mantles, as art objects rather than practical hunter's helpers. He takes orders and will carve a decorative piece, such as a miniature, if the customer wants one.

Buying a bird from Bill will set you back at least $200.

"Some I keep," he continued. "I'm not commercial. I make a decoy the best I can. I couldn't consider myself a master."

Bill signs and brands each bird that leaves the shop. If it's hollow, he'll seal in a handful of bird shot, which may be a trademark with him.

"I was probably the first one to put 'em in. Old-time decoys had shot in 'em from shooting cripples. That decoy my grandfather made's all shot up."

You'd say Bill had an advantage, with all his river time, in knowing what a duck ought to look like when you bring it out of a pine block. He had a chance to study hundreds and hundreds of birds, close-up.

A canvasback's the hardest to carve, in his opinion. "You have to have the head just right," he said. Bill's heads seem as if they just popped out of an egg.

Sure, he tries to make his ducks look like ducks.

How many had he carved, in all this time? Bill shrugged.

"I haven't the slightest idea. Never kept track. I only work when I feel like it. I never know what I'll do next."
– *1992*

Onchiota

I headed into Franklin County one bright and warm day last week with the notion of toasting the 100th anniversary of the Adirondack Park. This natural wonder of ours folds across nearly six million acres north of the Thruway.

I crossed the blue line, and before I knew it, I sat in a rusty folding chair in front of H.J. Tormey & Son Inc. sucking a can of beer and believing the park's full of surprises.

This is Onchiota, a three corners with a two-way stop about 10 miles north of Saranac Lake, as the bull flies.

Onchiota used to be bigger, no matter.

"There's not much doing, but we still have a lot of fun," Bing Tormey said to me after we shook hands.

The hamlet seems to revolve around Bing, Bing around it. His father bought the whole shooting match 70 years ago. He's the "*& Son*" on the sign. Mom called him Hayden.

Onchiota used to be one large sawmill town. Lately, it had a general store-post office, a grocery and 13 tourist cabins. Now it has Bing, his pals and a lot of fun, sometimes with the help of strangers such as me.

I put on the brakes of my car when I came up on "*Onchiota Irrational Airport.*"

There's more, lots of it.

Bing wondered if I'd noticed the sign for the Maple Berry Festival. I had, although "Ochi," as the place is called by Bing, has enough signs to keep your eyes moving 20 to 30 minutes. Even then you've missed a few. They're also stowed in the store, which held the IGA and Onchiota post office until eight years ago.

Bing was Postmaster, by the way. These days he sells firewood, carves duck decoys, drinks beer and pulls on your leg, real hard.

The sign reads, "*Onchiota Maple Berry Festival 1 p.m. Oct. 11.*"

"We'll have to go out and pin the berries on the trees," Lane Knight was saying. Lane, called "Brownie," is a former school teacher from Vermont who sells videos out of his home up the road.

Brownie likes to "blow up things" on his pond. He said he's planning to explode an inflatable Halloween skeleton for the trick-or-treaters this year.

We laughed. I said I might be a few minutes late on the 11th. Herb Rock said I'd probably miss the festival.

Herb's in from Lake Placid to lie to strangers. He retired as executive chef at Mirror Lake Inn a while ago.

The pals started talking about the graduate student from Plattsburgh who'd believed them when they told him you could plug lights into a currant bush. When he tried, they didn't work.

"Only if you have a negative attitude," Brownie said.

Herb asked if I noticed the Onchiota Interpretive

Center, yonder next to the trees? I turned around to see a converted outhouse.

"We had a coconut head in there with a sign, '*Meet Mr. Cuomo*'," Herb explained, "but somebody stole it."

"We used to have a toll booth, too," Brownie said. "We ought to put it back."

Cars and trucks zigged through, a few even observing the stop signs. Traffic's a challenge, Bing said, tugging on his Kushaqua Hunting Club cap. Kushaqua's another name for Rainbow Lake, which is nearby.

"I had a sign, *'Damn, Slow Down,'* but somebody took that, too."

Bing's firewood, tucked up to the roof of the store's front porch, whistles out of Onchiota. He met the thieves with a sign, of course. This one mentions that 10 of the sticks on the porch have dynamite in them.

Then you've got the Rainbow Lake Monster.

"We sat a paper-mache monster out on the bog," Bing explained. "Like that one at Lake Champlain."

We'd seen the piece on Champ, the Champlain creature, on television the other night. Someone had taken a snapshot of what looked like a dinosaur in the lake a few years back.

Bing told us the picture simply showed a family of otter, snaking in and out of the swells.

No kidding? No kidding, our host said. He'd seen them.

Just then a golden eagle glided in peaceable circles several hundred feet above Onchiota. We all looked into the cloudless blue of an anniversary sky.

"I hope he doesn't get hit by an incoming aircraft," Brownie said.

It turns out Brownie built the miniature airport across the road as a present to Bing. A surprise, actually. It sits in front of the abandoned cabins. The abandoned shuffleboard court's the runway.

Yes, that's a woodpecker pecking at a beer can on that whirlygig above the landing strip.

The other stuff? You figure them out.

Brownie also claimed responsibility for the carved beaver on top of the beaver lodge with a can of Bud raised to its lips. That's on his pond, too.

A young woman in a silver Honda braked her car at the stop sign. She waved at the pals, who had settled onto the front stoop. "Nice signs," she yelled. They waved back.

Bing's house is across the way, but you'll find him at the store most of the time, he said. Sometimes he'll sit out front at the folding table and have a meal, accompanied by a six-pack and Patsy, his beagle. He has a fireplace next to a wood pile when the meal's hot.

"My lunch," Bing said, pointing to two empty ears of corn on the table.

The pals got me inside the store to see Brownie's miniature of Bing at work in his shop. The night version has a light in it. I passed under a sign above the front door, "*Blood, Sweat & Beers Inc.*"

Bing had me check out another sign, this one tacked

to the far wall. I looked at a set of letters which might have been copied from the wall of a Pharaoh's tomb.

"Back up," Bing suggested. Herb wanted me to avoid the hole in the floor.

I backed up. The sign came into focus: "*No Sex Causes Bad Eyes.*"

We laughed.

When I noticed a few decoys on a shelf, Bing said he spent winters carving. He'd been encouraged into the hobby several years ago by the late Ken Harris of Woodville.

"I did 140 last year," Bing explained. "They're all gone."

Herb spoke up. "Bing taught me to carve," he said. "I do loons."

Before I left, I had one of Herb's loons and Bing's miniature carving of the Rainbow Lake Monster.

I also carried out a copy of Bing's booklet, "*The Legend of Lake Kushaqua, Onchiota, Rainbow Lake.*" This is his effort to explain the origin of the Iroquois word, Onchiota.

Herb's barber for Onchiota, too, he said.

"I cut everybody's hair," he explained. "Bing cuts mine. We do it out in front, when we can."

Airport, stop signs, interpretive center, wood pile, lunch table, barber, beavers drinking beer, a hometown industry: What more could a man ask of a place?

That's why Bing told me he never considered moving from the town where he was born 70 years ago, right up there in that room, above the old post office.

"I like it here," he said. - *1992*

Wolfe Island

I went to Wolfe Island to help observe its 200th birthday and found myself sitting on the veranda of the Woodman House and watching the ferry line form. A couple of weeks before, I was in the line.

This string of motor vehicles, milk trucks to mopeds, goes to the heart of Wolfe, which is the largest of the Thousand Islands and surely one of the most interesting. Islanders can't live without the boats, but the relationship's a difficult one.

Permanent residents — there are about 1,100 of them — have been known to take a tire iron to a stranger who tried to cut into the ferry line.

"Cars from Horne's Ferry continue to break into the line, causing anger and anguish," an item in a recent issue of the Wolfe Island Taxpayers Association Newsletter declared. *"Island residents are subject to waits that are totally unreasonable."*

"Look at that," Marg Woodman was saying. She got up and pointed to a car with New York plates. The driver tried to make a U-turn in the middle of King's Highway 96, the main drag of Marysville, and Wolfe Island.

"We've got signs '*Do Not Block Driveway,*' but nobody pays attention to them," Marg said. "We sit out here on Sunday night and watch the cars. The traffic's unbelievable. People talk about moving the ferry landing out of Marysville, down to the winter dock, but the settlement's here. I guess you train yourself to live with it."

The boats and the traffic, especially during summer months, are talked about a lot. So is "the development," a proposed retirement community at the head of the island which could add 5,000 citizens to the rolls.

Wolfe, which got its name from a British war hero, isn't the peaceable farming and fishing community it used to be. There's worry about that.

"The island is changing," Carmel Cosgrove said to me. She was born on Wolfe 80 years ago. Her 1830s house is on the main drag, too, a few lots upstreet from Marg Woodman.

"Everybody goes by and says, 'Hi, Carm,' but I don't know who they are," she said.

Bruce Woodman, Marg's husband, said the same thing: "I look at the boat lineup, and I only know every fourth person. The big problem about the ferry's always been here. Islanders live with it; it's the newcomers who've got a problem."

I'd gone to Wolfe because I knew there had to be more to the place than the 10-minute drive between the Horne Transportation ferry dock from Cape Vincent and the Ontario Department of Transport's ferry to Kingston. We'd made the trip many times on the way to Kingston.

My neighbor Jim Russell helped. His friends Betty

Ann and David Field of Toronto have a summer home in an old farm house a couple of miles out of Marysville, on the island's Kingston shoreline. Jim arranged a visit and before long I sat on the Woodmans' veranda, checking out cars and trucks circling into line on Route 96.

We chewed the fat about life on Wolfe: past, present and future.

Bruce Woodman's island, Marg's not. She's Kingston. His family — one of about 15 core kinship networks on Wolfe — has been here since the earliest settlement, before 1830.

They run Woodman House, a fishing resort opened by Bruce's father and grandfather in 1923. These days the sign says "*Bed and Breakfast,*" but a lot of the visitors are here because Bruce's one of the region's best-known fishing guides. He also carves duck decoys and catches fish for the market.

Bruce's traditional, in several ways, because he makes a living off the water and comes from island bloodlines. Most of the permanent residents — the numbers about triple when you add in summer cottagers — work off the island and commute by ferry.

Dairy farmers on the island decreased from 168 in 1965 to 22 this year. All of the cows milked here supply Wolfe's only other industry besides tourism, a Kraft Foods cheese plant that employs nine.

Marg Woodman told me she had trouble getting her husband to leave his home place, even to get a haircut.

Wolfe Island hasn't had its own barber in many years.

It also lacks a police department, full-time doctor, bank, high school, place to play hockey and shops, except for mom-and-pop groceries.

When I asked Bruce about that, he smiled. "Somebody has to stay home," he said.

Most of the land is farmed. Bruce figures maybe 90 percent of the citizens "are related, some way or other." Wolfe is 21 miles long.

Trouble is, islanders can't stay home, tied as they are to the Ontario mainland 25 minutes across the St. Lawrence River in Kingston. So, they fret over the long ferry lines, on both sides of the river, and the congestion in Marysville.

Perry Chesney, president of the taxpayers' group; Everett Hogan, a farmer; and Margaret Knott, who puts together the association's newsletter, joined us at the Woodmans. None of the neighbors seemed to be able to explain the ferry traffic outbreak. They await a study by the provincial government.

Is it more summer residents? Yes, although the character of the off-islanders changes, from American to Canadian.

Is it more islanders? Not more islanders, but more commuting. And more two-car families. Wolfe's population peaked at 3,601 in 1861, when lumbering and quarrying provided jobs.

"The boats are full but not with American plates," Perry said. He commutes to Kingston every day to work in the post office.

Marg Woodman's theory has to do with Kingston citizens who ride the ferry for a lark in their cars. "When they get here, they find out there's nothing much to do, so they turn around and go home," she said.

The government's solutions include adding another boat (there's only one and a second craft, outfitted and ready to go, is called too expensive to operate), moving the ferry dock, a new schedule, charging a fare (the Horne line, operated by another long-time island family, has a fee; the Kingston run doesn't) or even a bridge.

Folks I talked to said they'd never live to see a bridge to Kingston but they felt the "development," officially The Landings at Wolfe Island, wouldn't happen without an improvement in the Kingston ferry service.

Of course, there's disagreement on the island about whether the complex of 1,400 new homes, a golf course, hotel, marina, air strip, shops and restaurants ought to happen at all.

The project must pass a series of government approvals, on and off the island.

Opinions split on whether Wolfe can survive a fivefold increase in its population. Or even if the island can survive without it.

Margaret Knott, who's lived here four years, said the issue was summed up by an islander who said to her, "In my heart, I don't want change, but I know it has to happen."

Some older residents think the new complex, proposed by the Matthews Group, Ltd. of Toronto, would bring jobs. Jobs would keep their children in the home place.

"If it comes on line," Perry explained, "we want it so it benefits all the islanders. We don't know that yet. People have to have answers."

Margaret said she and her husband, Walter, a broadcasting executive who commutes, picked Wolfe as their new home because of what it was, not what it might be on the site plan in the town hall.

"We like it the way it is," she said.

The Knotts have lived all over Canada. They moved to Ontario from the West. Margaret said she'd seen developments similar to The Landings elsewhere; the impact on Wolfe concerned her.

"They take control and isolate the existing community," she explained. "They have everything they want right there."

The others agreed. Wolfe has no sewer, water or garbage disposal systems, other than the town dump where refuse is burned in an old quarry near the cheese plant. The Landings would have all of those services, and more.

I asked Bruce Woodman what he thought the answer was. "Not to have a development," he said, poking his cigar stump in the air. "We need some tax base, but that would change the whole island."

Down the way, Carmel Cosgrove sat in a battered lawn chair, with her cane leaning against the clapboards, and looked out across her yard to the ferry line, and Kingston, twinkling at the horizon. What did she make of this deal of Matthews?

"A pipe dream" she snorted. "Bruce will have a bridge to town before they do that."

<>

The river's right up under Bruce Woodman's house, in the center of the village where the St. Lawrence licks at Wolfe Island. That's as it should be. Bruce's a river rat — proud to be it, too.

One of the things about a river rat is that it's hard separating him from the water he's seen, felt and listened to since the day he was born.

Bruce and his wife, Margaret, live in a house that rests over the edge of one of Marysville's rocky beaches.

"We built the cottage because Bruce didn't want to get any farther away from the water," Margaret tells me.

She came to the island to live "and made it special" after the Woodmans married in 1955.

I dropped in on the Woodmans on the Saturday morning in August when the island had everybody involved in the annual Country Fest. There'd been a parade — I watched from in front of Fargo's General Store — and then the booths opened at the fairgrounds up at the end of Victoria Street.

The Woodmans had moved their lawn chairs into the boathouse after the parade. The dock's under the living room. The day before, I joined Margaret — the island's first female town councilor — for a chat on the veranda of Woodman House.

I followed Bruce into his workshop. Benches and shelves are lined with his decoys, made of wood. Bruce lit his cigar stub.

Yes, he said, likely he's the last of the traditional carvers, who make birds for decoys, not decorations. There aren't that many left on all of the Thousand Islands, in fact. Wolfe's the largest of them, 21 miles head to foot, and 7 miles wide.

As we talked, I measured Bruce a contented man. He knows where he's at, and he likes it there. He's not even that worried, as some islanders seem to be, about heavy traffic on the Kingston ferry. I mentioned what Margaret told me about haircuts. He drew a glow to his stub.

"The only thing that takes the young people away is job security," he said. As if to emphasize the point, Barry Woodman appeared. He works for his dad but spent five years in Montreal and Toronto.

Barry nodded his head at what Bruce said. "I'll never leave again," he said.

The sense that Wolfe's something special sticks with the visitor.

Neighbor Margaret Knott told me about what she sees as the time warp of the island: "life here's the same as it was 25 years ago."

She mentioned the popularity of the county library branch behind the town hall in Marysville. Islanders read a lot. They're also up on things. If you start a conversation on politics, Margaret warned, you'd better know what you're talking about.

Folks listen to the radio more than they watch television. The Kingston station has a relay unit near Marysville. Mary was Mrs. Archibald Hitchcock, who was born here in 1789, was postmistress and died in 1877.

Margaret drove me around the island's head, near the former Union Carbide executive retreat where a new development could unfold across peaceable farm fields, bays and marshes.

"Is this incredible?" Margaret asked at one point, looking out at Reed's Bay. We turned onto the start of Route 96 and passed the ferry landing where a boat takes two cars and several walkers and bike-riders to Simcoe Island on a cable pull.

Margaret pointed out where the scenic highway's being widened. Was this the future? Two-lane roads spinning into a sparkling, self-contained "recreational community?"

"I've been a few places, but I doubt I'll live anywhere else," she said.

She took me to see Capt. R.F. Fawcett at this farm house near the old canal and the winter dock. I heard almost the same words, from a distinguished river rat whose family's been here 150 years.

R.F.'s retired from ferry service. He ran the operation and skippered the *Wolfe Islander III* back and forth from home to Kingston. "I'm the only one left who brought her out of the shipyard in November 1946," he said.

Fawcetts farmed it, the way most of the long-lived families did. The Captain still keeps a herd of Herefords. He sold a few lots on the shoreline, too. Early on, they had limestone quarries and lumbering on Wolfe.

These days, just 22 farmers bring their milk to the Kraft Foods plant in Marysville, where it's processed into feta cheese. If they're not farming or living off the water and tourists, islanders have to take the ferry to Kingston to work.

R.F. fishes commercially in retirement. He said there are eight fishermen left, including Bruce Woodman. They take out their nets and bring back bullheads, perch, eels and sunfish. "Most of them end up in Europe," R.F. explained.

Would he leave the island? The Captain looked at me in a way that suggested it was a dumb question.

"Sure, I've been off the island a lot in my life," he replied. "But I always came back. I've been all over the country, and there's no place better than this."

Wolfe's wide at the head, at the west, and narrows to a point of land at the east. Route 96 stretches the 21 miles, with Route 95 as a belt from Horne's Point, the ferry landing, to Marysville.

Almost everything east of the hamlet's in farming. I drove a few miles before another car passed. On the way to the foot, I passed a quiet country chapel, Christ Church, with a quiet country cemetery next door. Huge rolled bales of hay seemed to be everywhere.

Everett Hogan runs one of the 20-odd farms left on Wolfe. He told me there's always been something special about the island's hay; this year it's a "notorious crop," in his opinion. The rain that kept tourists off the island made the sum and substance of dairy farming grow like crazy.

Everett's great-grandfather came from Ireland. He's here because he's island-born. He makes a living, and it's quiet. Yes, he likes the quiet.

Carmel Cosgrove and I talked on her front stoop in Marysville after the parade. She lives in Kingston, retired as a nurse at the shipyard, but Wolfe's home, where she was born, where her ancestors lived. Her late brother, Winston, wrote the island history published in 1973.

We watched the cars loop around to join the ferry line, and Carmel talked about her Great Aunt Caroline Spoor, who once owned all the land hereabouts. Carmel's house belonged to Caroline's servants and to a cobbler after that. The shoe man had a wooden leg from the Boer War.

Carmel's talk is salted with words of four letters, and more. She doesn't think "the development" will happen. But she knows Wolfe changes, almost before her eyes.

"Used to be farmers married farmers' daughters," she said. "Now the men marry town girls, and they don't want to live here."

George Horne's another carrier of island tradition. He's the skipper who pilots us on the *William Darrell* ferry between The Cape and Horne's Point May to October — 2,800 trips a season. The boat's named for Darrell Horne, his father, and William, his uncle. They built it in 1953.

Kinsmen, either Hornes or Hinckleys, have been carrying vehicles and passengers across this 10 minutes of river since 1829. George's partner is his brother, Bruce. The

Hornes are Wolfe Island, of course.

So is Andrea Dean. I read her essay about the home place on the wall of Wolfe Island School during Country Fest. The child's words sum up what it's like to be here:

"How would you like it if your parents took you away from Wolfe Island? Mine did, when I was in kindergarten. But they brought me back.

"I live on Wolfe Island because it's nice to live here. My dad works at Don McDonald's (farm). It is on the island. I have a house on the road to the winter dock. I'm glad I live on Wolfe Island." - 1992

The Five and Dime

Quickly, before the colors fade, we need to take a last look at F.W. Woolworth Co., our first great retail chain.

This American landmark is about to disappear, forever. The last 400 Woolworths will close before the end of the year.

Where better to glimpse the shadows of Frank Winfield Woolworth than in Jefferson County, where F.W. was born, where he birthed the 5- and 10-cent business more than a century ago.

That's why I'm standing in a park with a fountain in Public Square, Watertown, looking at a lot in the city's downtown where it all began. I'm looking at the Woolworth Building, six stories of it, and a red neon sign in a storefront at what the Woolworth people used to call the "American Corner."

The sign is interesting, when we consider this is the corner where F.W., then a young shop assistant at a Watertown general store, watched customers quickly buy household items from a table the owners had marked 5 cents each.

That was in 1878, when he'd just left his father's farm a dozen miles to the east at Great Bend. He didn't want to be a farmer. Instead, he would open his own store, where everything cost a nickel.

He did, the next year, in Utica. His first "*Great 5-Cent Store*" failed, but he tried again later the same year, that time in Lancaster, Pa.

Yes, we know the rest of the story...

F.W. shortly returned to Watertown as a partner with his former bosses, the Moores, in a new "5 and 10-cent" store at the old stand on the corner. The present Woolworth Building went up on the site in 1921, eight years after the New York City skyscraper with the same name.

It was the corporate headquarters and the world's tallest building, back then.

The company held its annual meetings at the American Corner in Watertown until 1966.

In 1971, the store was moved across Arsenal Street, as the anchor of a new downtown mall. The landmark block was donated to Henry Keep senior home. It's in foreclosure, and on the market, through the owner, Carthage Savings and Loan.

Tim O'Brien at Prudential Crown Realty said Friday the bank has two interested buyers and the prospect of city grants, which could mean new life on the corner.

The bulb's dim this week. Most of the fronts are empty, or boarded. The directory in the lobby lists 17 tenants, about the number of offices available on one of the six floors.

That single retail tenant at the corner jumps out: It's a Dollar Depot.

"*Everything Is $1.00,*" the sign reads. F.W. might

approve of how his landmark has come around to face its own history.

Watertown, it turns out, has yet another claim to retail fame: Next door to the Woolworth Building is Paddock Arcade, said to be "the oldest covered mall in the United States."

I head for Woolworth's, passing more empty spaces, including a bar named "*Clueless.*"

The mall parking lot is ample, but not with parkers. On one side, the only citizen in sight is a lonely kid on a skateboard.

Another interesting sign waves across the Woolworth front: *"Entire Store on Sale."*

I pick up a flier: *"After 118 years...Woolworth's Biggest Sale Ever."* I'll say.

This flagship store has 65 full- and part-time workers. They don't know when Woolworth's Watertown will close; it will take a while for the liquidators, who are already at work, to sell the place down to the fixtures.

The lunch counter — Harvest House Coffee Shop — home to those chocolate malts and grilled cheese sandwiches, was scheduled to close Saturday.

On the wall next to Books, I find a small historical display, moved from across the street in 1971. It tells us *"Watertown is the birthplace of the 5-cent sales concept."*

The books are 10 percent off. The goldfish in Pets are gone, but there are still parakeets at $16.99 each.

Around the square is Washington Street and the mansion that's home to the Jefferson County Historical Society.

I'm greeted by a larger-than-life bronze bust of F.W., staring down at me from the top of the second-floor stairway, and director Fred Rollins, who has his feet on the floor.

We sit in the library while I go through the society's large file of Woolworth memorabilia, including the program for the company's 25th anniversary bash, at Utica Auditorium, in 1904.

Fred tells me he thinks the end of Woolworth's is a tough blow to the founder's hometown. At the peak, just five years ago, Woolworth's sales reached $9.9 billion, with 8,386 stores around the world.

"I was in the store the day after the announcement (July 17) and I felt an incredible sadness," he said.

Sally Conway said she's sad, too. She'd been checking out the sales at Woolworth's Watertown; the sense of passage is strong. Her late husband, Edison, worked at the old store as a window designer for 47 years.

Sally, who grew up in Black River, has been a Woolworth customer, proudly, "since I opened my eyes." As a kid, she went to the lunch counter for ice cream, and "my kid sister ordered mashed potatoes and gravy."

As a grown-up, working across Public Square, she recalls the double line of folks waiting to grab a stool for lunch, perhaps feasting on a 25-cent turkey dinner or one of Emma Franklin's famed pumpkin pies.

Sally told me it's hard to figure what happened to the world's grandest store chain, "but I'm not convinced they couldn't make it."

And what of her husband, who died in 1996? "I'm so glad he is not here to see this," Sally said. "He would break down and cry."

The gem of Fred's collections at the historical society, as far as he's concerned, is the store directory saved from the old Woolworth's in Watertown. It's a time frame, stopped at 1970:

Appliances, yard goods, shower curtains, luggage, TVs, ribbons, hobbies, clocks, wigs....

Frank Woolworth and his younger brother, Charles Sumner Woolworth, were born on a remote farm — his grandfather's — near the hamlet of East Rodman, south of Watertown. The house is gone.

By the time he died, nearly 90 years later, "Sum" Woolworth, like his brother, would be one of the world's richest men. He served as vice president of the corporation, along with Seymour Knox, his cousin from the St. Lawrence County hamlet of Russell, and a pal from Brownsville, Fred Kirby.

F.W., who lived like the merchant prince he became, never lost touch with his North Country roots, according to Helen Fargo of Great Bend. I met with Helen and Sue Wiley, the town of Champion historian, in a landmark that speaks to that loyalty.

In 1915, the millionaire's Methodist friends in Great Bend started attending the new church he gave them, in the hamlet where Route 3 passes the great bend of the Black River. Woolworth Memorial United Methodist Church's handsome New England spire is the tallest landmark for miles.

By that time, F.W. had a nifty mansion at Glen Cove, on the Long Island Sound. When that burned in 1916, he rebuilt quickly — bigger and better.

Winfield Hall remains a landmark among the big houses of Nassau County. It's owned by Pall Corp. and not used at the moment, according to Louise Tripoli, at Glen Cove City Hall.

Glen Cove also has one of the remnant 400 Woolworth's, where Louise told me she has bought "hundreds of goldfish and other little things" over the years. Yes, she is sad, as well.

Syracuse once had two Woolworth's at the same time, within blocks of each other: one at 327 S. Salina St. (now Rite Aid, with the five-and-dime facade partially hidden) and one at 242 N. Salina St., in the very block where I write this column.

The last Onondaga County Woolworth's faded at Shoppingtown a couple of years ago.

Helen Fargo, historian of the Woolworth church, shared a small collection of F.W. documents in the church archives, including letters he wrote to Great Bend friends who wanted him to help them with a new church.

In 1911, he wrote to Cordelia Pennock, *"I might be induced to do something"* on a lot he owned at the corner. He'd get back to them. When he did, according to another letter, F.W. promised *"no more than $8,000."*

Later, they compromised on $22,000, according to Helen, which gave Great Bend not only a church, but a parsonage and two carriage barns. F.W. threw in a bonus of $20,000 in bonds, the interest to be used for upkeep.

The gift continues, Helen said.

Every year, church trustees get a check for $2,000 from the Winfield Foundation — the Woolworth family foundation — for maintenance. The most recent arrived but two weeks ago.

Another letter, on Winfield Hall stationary, thanks the Sunday school children at the church for sending wood flowers and violets they'd gathered to F.W. three years before he died at Glen Cove at the age of 67.

Sue Wiley, who has been historian of the town since 1974, shared the story she'd heard from older residents that during F.W.'s lifetime, "attendance at the Sunday school, where he'd gone himself, was very high."

One reason? The merchant prince got a gift list from the children each Christmas and filled it with toys from the stores.

Helen and Sue also know, by tradition, that F.W. helped people in the hamlet where he'd lived when they had financial challenges. He found jobs for some with the company.

In 1926, his two surviving daughters — another, Edna, who died young, was the mother of Woolworth heiress Barbara Hutton — gave Great Bend land for a village green. In his own time, F.W. provided the community with new sidewalks and maple trees to line the streets.

Sue took me down the road toward Champion, passing the old Woolworth farm, to Sunnyside Cemetery, where F.W.'s parents, John and Fanny, and an aunt are buried beside a monument that's taller than any other there.

F.W., his wife, Jenny, and other family members, including Barbara Hutton, lie in a $100,000 mausoleum in Woodlawn Cemetery, Brooklyn.

"He never, never lost touch with Great Bend, even to the end of his life," Helen said. - *1997*

Grampa Moses

Seth Moulton got a late start as a working artist, but he caught up fast.

By the time he died in 1971 at the age of 82, he'd turned out more than 400 paintings, most of them on parchment, some on whatever he had handy, including tablecloths. Seth was a retired farmer who lived outside the St. Lawrence County hamlet of Winthrop on the St. Regis River.

He called himself "Grampa Moses of the North Country."

Most of Seth's small-town masterworks of storytelling stayed in the family. He'd give away a painting, but never sell it, no sir.

Besides his sense of humor, which was sharp as a stick, he had this Yankee stubbornness.

One time he painted a picture for Nelson Rockefeller. When he was asked to mail it, rather than giving it to the governor in Winthrop, Seth said, forget it.

I met Seth in 1969. My wife, Sandy, and I visited him then, when I was working on an article about his new life as an artist.

About a month ago I found Seth's *"Fat Girl Picking Butternuts"* in a Syracuse flea market. I bought the painting and last week took it home to Winthrop.

Most of the life's work of the farmer-artist stayed in cardboard boxes in his daughter Bessie Kline's house, where Seth lived in retirement. When Bessie moved to Florida, the boxes went to her daughter's place.

When Meredith Fayette, Seth's granddaughter, left for Florida herself, a rediscovery took place in the town of Stockholm, where Seth spent his last 40 years.

"People around here had pretty much forgotten about him," Vicki Martin of the Stockholm Historical Organization explained last week. "We thought the paintings were gone, destroyed."

Not at all. Seth Moulton comes to life in a very special way this weekend in Winthrop.

Last fall, Meredith Fayette donated 228 original Moultons to the historical group that didn't exist in her grandfather's time. The paintings will be shown in public for the first time in the organization's history center, in Stockholm Town Hall, on Route 11-C.

More showings are planned next year, including one at the St. Lawrence County Historical Association museum in Canton.

I visited the history center last week as Vicki Martin and other volunteers worked to transform the town justice courtroom into a weekend art gallery.

The helpers included Vicki's sister, Patsy McGraw; Dottie and Carl Goodrich, Carelton Stickney and Cathy Hance.

I marveled at the enthusiasm of the helpers and what they've accomplished by way of building a museum and a collection of artifacts and documents since they formed in 1979.

Carleton Stickney, one of the founders, showed me around, including where the historians re-created a school room, Victorian parlor, general store and room from a pioneer log house.

"It's a lot of work, but we have a lot of fun," Carleton said.

Pat Furgison is the court clerk in Winthrop. She's also president of the organization. She'd known Meredith Fayette growing up, and Meredith came to her with the idea of donating the paintings.

"She said she was moving and wanted to know if we'd like the paintings for the museum. I said 'Sure.' I think we knew right away we wanted to have an exhibit."

Pat also recalls the warm summer day in 1997 when she and a friend started leafing through Seth's paintings. The Moulton archive was in good shape after 26 years, just "a little dusty."

As the paintings were shared with other members, they say their eyes widened at the variety of Seth's work and the quantity.

"We were knocked over," Vicki Martin said. She's a former school teacher from Texas who moved to Stockholm with her husband the year after Seth died. Vicki is the archivist of the county historical association.

"We knew we really had something," she said.

Others agreed, including Diana Cooper, curator of the art collection at Potsdam College, who helped get the paintings in shape.

The rest, they did themselves, including the Burma Shave signs greeting visitors outside the museum that capture the spirit of Seth's eccentric spelling. One points the way to *"Seth's art exabision."*

Patsy McGraw did the catalog, which includes a short biography of Seth. None of the folks involved in the exhibit knew Seth, except Loren Furgison, Pat's husband, who called him "quite a fellow, sure was."

Patsy said volunteers feel they know Seth after reading his letters and checking out the legends he wrote on his paintings.

"Seth really puts you in a good mood," she remarked.

A sampling of painting titles explains their appeal: *"For Runners of Shopping Centers"* (peddlers), *"Newly Weds Pulling Together"* (tethered horses going in opposite directions) and *"Fat Girl Picking Butternuts"* (painted in 1959 and exposing a naked rear end).

Vicki Martin believes Seth, who seldom exhibited his paintings, would like this hometown show.

"We're trying to do it right by him," she explained. "After all is said and done, I think he'd rather be here than with the *'expurts'.*" - *1998*

Buster Bird

I was in Thendara, a suburb of Old Forge, visiting with one of New York's well-preserved natural resources the other day.

His name is Norton Bird — please call him "Buster" or "Bus" — and he just turned 91.

Bus is a retired bush pilot. He's also an Adirondacker, former wilderness guide, ace mechanic, founder of Bird's Seaplane Service at Inlet, husband to four wives and, as of this month, the subject of a children's book.

And he's just about finished with his own memoir of nearly a century living up close and personal with the 6 million acres of public park we call the Adirondacks.

"I know the country. I have a pretty good description of it," Bus said as we sat with his wife Irene in their living room and took extreme pleasure from a view of the North Branch of the Moose River across the yard.

Nuthatches fluttered at the feeders, and a pair of otters splashed in the river, props of the sort of glorious fall day the Adirondacks were invented for.

Bus was talking about what it takes to be a bush pilot, an adventurer who flies small planes into remote areas.

"You need to know where you are every minute, where the mountains are," he said. "You rely on your own judgment, not a map. When I started, all we had was a compass in the plane. You know enough not to fly into crud. You have mental maps in your mind."

Bus got a license to fly and bought his first plane — a Cessna 140 — in 1948, working off Sixth Lake, Inlet. The feds forced him to retire because of his age in 1992. By then, he'd logged 24,000 hours of flight time, most of that above the mountains he was born into.

That would make him owner of the most intimate knowledge of the Adirondacks in the universe, because he also worked as a guide from age 14.

He's not shy about mentioning "all the great people" he has met on the ground and above it and from 20 years of politics in Inlet and Hamilton County. One special treat was the Charles Taylor Award he got three years ago, recognizing 50 years of skill as an airplane mechanic.

The man's also excited about "all the fuss over the book" by Wendy Cheyette Lewison, a summer visitor to Inlet and author of more than 50 children's books.

It's called "*Buzz the Little Seaplane*," and the pilot is a guy named Buster Bird.

Bus is amused by the book, too, in which he co-stars with a seaplane with more personality than the ones at the dock at Inlet.

Bus admits he assessed the story "a crazy damned thing" when he first read Lewison's manuscript. "It's a children's book," he says. "It may not make sense to an adult."

There are a few rusty technical details, according to

Bus, including the illustration that shows the pilot on the wrong side of the plane, and the one of fighting a forest fire with a hose hooked to the aircraft from the ground.

How the heck do you do that?

Not that our man didn't get close to water lines now and again, especially when the Birds had a contract to "plant fish" in a few, or all, of the Adirondacks' 3,000 lakes and ponds. That meant flushing thousands of fingerlings and a stream of water down a "stove pipe" from 100 feet up.

Things are different now for Bus's son, Don, a jet engineer who flies the Bird fleet of two seaplanes. Back when, Bus was all over the park on jobs ranging from ferrying rich people to a favorite restaurant to spotting fires, to scattering human ashes.

The bread-and-butter work for Buster was flying hunters and fishermen into remote lakes and campsites, a profitable job the blankety-blank Adirondack Park Agency legislated the Birds out of years ago. Most of the lakes and ponds now are off-limits to aircraft.

"The environmentalists want you to walk in," Bus says grumpily.

That means Adirondack pilots also can't fly fire surveillance or search and rescue, except in special cases when the state calls for help.

Bus shook his head, wondering at the fate of a camper back there with a broken leg, hot appendix or heart attack, waiting for rescuers to walk him out of the woods.

Oh, well. "You change. We do more charters now,"

and scenic tours, he explained.

There was a time the Birds had five planes. Now there are two, and two pilots, since Bus stepped down. He's still manager, although he and Irene spend the winter in Florida, leaving Thendara "right after we vote on Election Day."

There have been Birds on the ground in the Adirondacks since the 1880s, when Bus's grandfather, Edward, migrated from Vermont to "work the hotels and guide" at Blue Mountain Lake. Bus's dad was Norton, an engineer on the Raquette Lake Railroad until it closed in 1934. Some Birds are still in Raquette: Bus's nephew Dick has Bird's Boat Livery.

"You never leave one lake until you know you can make it to the next one. Sometimes you had to camp overnight. My father taught me to survive in the bush. I always carry a tent, hatchet, rifle, shovel and two candy bars. You just dig a hole and make yourself a snow house."

Bus busts with stories. Some he plans to put in the book he's working up with a writer friend.

He'll say, while he thinks the "old-fashioned ways were the best," he knows "things are a lot better now." He may mention that, while he has no regrets over how he spent 44 years, he won't recommend bush-piloting to his grandkids "because of all the close calls."

Bus shares the thrill a man gets alone in his flying machine, drifting above the trees and water, picking out something different every time he throttles off the water and into the clouds.

"I always figured I was a lot closer to the Lord when I was up there," he says. - *1999*

A Crowning Glory

They say faith moves mountains. Maybe it moves fire towers, too.

As obsessions go, Kermit Remele's is a modest one. He decided to save the 60-foot fire tower on Tooley Pond Mountain, north of Cranberry Lake when the state abandoned it.

It took him and his helpers close to 30 years, but the job's done.

"Kerm," as he's known to friends, will be at the state Ranger School in Wanakena this weekend for dedication of the relocated tower; now it rises from Cathedral Rock on the state College of Environmental Science and Forestry campus in St. Lawrence County.

Kerm took me to the top of that tower one sunny morning last week.

My host spent 30 years teaching forestry and surveying at the school, retiring in 1991. He's an adopted Adirondacker who grew up in Syracuse's Elmwood neighborhood and first saw the western Adirondacks plateau region as a ranger school student in 1942.

Kerm's brass belt buckle reads "surveyor." He's also a bush pilot and poet.

And dedicated to this fire tower.

"I knew the tower at Tooley Pond and I knew the last tower man," Kerm recalls as we leave his pickup truck and hike to the edge of Cathedral Rock where the tower's anchored.

"When I heard they were ready to take it down, it seemed a shame to let it go. We got some people together. It took us three weekends to get it down in pretty jig time."

One of the helpers in 1971 was Larry Rathman, a student who got his classmates to pitch in. Larry's still at Wanakena, as maintenance supervisor. He's Kerm's main man on the restoration project.

A few of the 1917 steel towers remain on Adirondack park peaks and lesser mountains since the state decided to spot fires from airplanes. (The original fire towers were made of logs and planks.) Most were taken out by helicopter. Those that survive are treated as landmarks, some of them looked after by "friends" groups.

The Tooley tower got a tender time-wrap in 1971. Wanakena crews removed each of the pieces, marked and stowed them in a barn at the school, where they rested more than two decades.

"We had plenty else to do," Kerm remarks.

Truth was, there needed to be a road to Cathedral Rock, at the northwest corner of the campus. The huge Adirondack boulder rises out of James Dubuar Forest, named for the longtime director of the ranger school.

"The students worked on it year to year but it took a long time," Kerm explained. Reconstruction got more serious after he retired and the volunteers had a way up to the spot at the top of the rock where they wanted to raise the tower.

Kerm says the site then was cleared and surveyed and "we lugged the steel" to the summit, where it was reassembled, from the base to the "box" or tower cab. "It went up much more slowly than it came down," he said.

Most of the original Aero Motor Co. framework got used. Even a few of the old window panes in the box survived. Although most of the work was volunteered by school alumni, staff and students, the college paid for new lumber for the stairs and cab floor.

He points to the roof, where beams of light dance off reflective metal plates.

"That's the crowning glory," Kerm says with a proud little smile.

This surveyor of the 21st century is a fan of a colleague from the 19th, a legendary mapmaker named Verplanck Colvin, who did the first survey of our Great North Woods at the end of the 1800s.

My guide's a founder of the "*Colvin Crew*," that's a small troop of Verplanck enthusiasts who want to retrace the master's footsteps through the Adirondacks. They climb mountains looking for the brass monument markers the first Colvin crews left.

"We'd also like to memorialize him in a better way than he's been so far," Kerm adds.

Cathedral Rock fire tower's a start. That crowning glory Kerm mentioned is a replica of one of Colvin's 19th century tin and wire "stan-helios," a device invented by the surveyor to spin in the wind and reflect sunlight that serves as back-sights for precise triangulation surveying.

The new stan-helio was designed and built of stainless steel by Paul Peacock of Wanakena, a retired master metal worker. Paul's dad, Roy, graduated in the first class of Wanakena rangers in 1912.

When we get to the top, I can't fault Kerm for wanting this tower back on solid rock; the view's worth 30 years of patience.

The ranger campus with its 40 students who study intensively for 31 weeks sits at the edge of the west inlet of Cranberry Lake, a dammed flow created years ago when cutting and milling timber was the work at Wanakena. Kerm's home is on the flow, too.

Through the windows we catch views of Cat Mountain, Indian Mountain, Dead Creek Flow, Route 3 snaking through the forest, even the outlines of the high peaks, about 40 miles to the east.

As we walk down, Kerm guides me along a path to another edge of the rock, this one facing east. Wanakena's name for this is "Lookout." Students built a log lean-to for the 100th anniversary of the Adirondack Park.

He and his wife, Mary Ann, were married at the lookout one May morning in 1982. "At dawn," Kerm says.

Back at the school, this poet of Wanakena shares a copy of the dedication poem he called "*Cathedral Rock.*" It ends:

"Where road now eases to/ A higher granite base,/ To student steel rising in a giddy climb,/To show in panoramic grace,/ Far greater heights just waiting to be trod." - 2000

The Dunes

Barbara Kilby has an apt way of saying what it means to spend 75 summers on the eastern Lake Ontario dunes in Jefferson County.

"It's something like sand in your shoes," she says. "It's hard to shake it out."

Barbara, a retired licensed practical nurse from Syracuse, has lived as many as seven months of the year in a small, isolated summer neighborhood of about 40 summer homes north of Sandy Pond. Montario Point — named for the first settler on the beach, Syracusan Fred Montayne — is near the midpoint of a system of barrier dunes stretching 16.5 miles, from the Salmon River to Black Pond, close by Henderson Harbor.

"A blessed place," according to Barbara, whose house sits on land her grandparents, Nellie and Albert Kilby, bought in the 1920s.

"The Indians called it their Garden of Eden," she adds.

This blessed garden on a strip of sand between the lake and a marshy pond is a troubled Eden, too. It's battered by wind, water and humans who want to live and play on the sand.

"Plenty of dynamics at work here," that's according to Randall Korman, a Syracuse University professor of architecture who summers with his family across the lawn from the Kilby place.

Among them: property owners, visitors, sport fishermen, marina operators, tourist advocates, users of the Ontario-St. Lawrence shipping channel; international, federal, state and local regulators and preservation groups, not to mention birds and other animals and natural forces.

"The real controller here is nature," says Sandy Bonnano of Nature Conservancy's office in Pulaski. Sandy's a dune ecologist, a recruit in a growing squad of conservation-minded folks who want to preserve the largest fresh water sand dune formation in New York.

Randall Korman's wife, Cheryl Gressani, is a preservation recruit, too. When she's not in Syracuse working for the Metropolitan Development Association, Cheryl's on the beach picking up litter, warning strangers off dunes and working with shore groups to meet the challenges of man and nature.

Almost 60 percent of the eastern Ontario dunes are privately owned, mostly by summer cottagers. The rest is protected public land, including Southwick Beach State Park and Lakeview Marsh Wildlife Management Area, which touches Montario Point.

In 1919, a dairy farmer named Thomas Colwell sold the shoreline where his cows grazed to "Fritz" Montayne, a real estate developer who once owned Rainbow Shores. Fritz moved into the old farmhouse and a colony developed, lot by lot.

At the Point, and elsewhere along the dunes in the '30s and '40s, farmers sold lake lots, and dunes were flattened for camps. Some campers planted grass, and flower beds, just like back home.

Man's footprints began to show.

Later, when Southwick Park opened, and later boat launch sites on public land, day visitors found their way to the sand. More footprints ... and later paw prints, tire tracks, dead campfires and trash, both beach litter and debris tossed up by the lake.

Cheryl Gressani says man and nature may live together, with lots of TLC.

"My son is the fourth generation here," Cheryl said the other day on the deck of the home she and Randall have been raising on posts above a secondary dune the last 14 years. "I feel we are stewards of the dunes. I found my calling to somehow protect the shoreline."

Randall Korman took care, and time, creating their new home on the beach. It's back from the point where Cheryl's grandparents and parents had their place. The handsome cedar house is among trees and beach grass with a long wall of windows to the lake.

Randall concedes nature and people collide, but adds "they can coexist, by education."

The New York Sea Grant program out of Oswego State College is involved, as well as a group of more than 30 public and private agencies called Ontario Dune Coalition.

Sally Sessler, a retired Syracuse University librarian

who lives in a 50-year family camp at North Rainbow Shores, chairs the private landowners committee of the coalition. Experts call these folks "riparians."

"I think we have to begin to keep what we have," Sally explains. The Sesslers, like other owners, are trying to replant sea grasses.

Scientists at Hobart and William Smith Colleges have been studying this barrier for three years; an early finding is that no more sand is coming into the system.

Barbara Kilby remembers "a beach the size of a football field" when she was a kid. Hurricane Agnes hammered down dunes in 1973. The Seaway had an influence, too — just how much is argued along the shoreline. Marina owners like high water, cottagers low.

Heavy summer rain and other factors give the folks at Montario tiny strips of beach this season. The narrower the beach, the closer the footprints to the dunes.

Barbara Kilby ran out of her family's cottage during a 1993 tornado that crashed huge trees into the place, destroying it. She rebuilt on the same lot, vowing to come back every summer "for as long as I can," while understanding this sand isn't hers.

"We don't own any of this," Barbara says. "We just get to use it. At least, we can leave it the way we found it." - *2000*

The Scotts

The big red, white and blue Mobil sign defines the main drag — Route 178 — in the Jefferson County hamlet of Henderson.

The folks under the sign define Henderson. The Scotts have been pumping gas, fixing flat tires and weary car engines, and running an unofficial community center here for 75 years.

Vic Scott opened his garage in 1926. His twin sons, Murray and Merrill, have had it ever since their dad died 40 years ago.

Scott's Garage is a landmark in this community two miles east of Henderson Harbor and Lake Ontario. Folks thereabouts call Henderson "the village," even though it's not, legally; the summer settlement next to the water is "The Harbor."

The Scotts are identical. Merrill lives in the 1827 house next to the garage with the Mobil Pegasus sign in his yard. Murray is across the street next to the North Branch of Stony Creek. He's 15 minutes older.

Townspeople call them "the Scott boys." Merrill and Murray will be 75 this fall.

Last month, Mobil recognized the family with a plaque engraved with the words *"outstanding service, loyalty and dedication."* The brothers say no one else at the awards ceremony in Syracuse was even close to their record of years selling Mobil products.

Scott's Garage seems at the center of things on a short main street that includes the Henderson Hotel, a liquor store, a general store, a gift shop, a post office, a fire barn and free library, a Methodist church, the vacant Henderson jailhouse, and a park built around the old mill pond.

Henderson was named for William, who owned the original tract. The hamlet's original name was "Salisbury Mills," for the mill that stood on the creek until 1963.

Henderson the town is home to several large farms, about 1,300 full-time citizens (5,000 to 6,000 in the summer) and a healthy fishing and tourist industry.

Murray mentions that the town seems to be growing, with a longer fishing season and an increase of population from the Fort Drum expansion and the state prison near Watertown.

The brothers are glad to hand out literature about the area along with a fill-up and windshield wipe, give directions and point to the faucet where campers may fill their water jugs — on the house. Raw lake and well water isn't recommended for drinking.

Murray and Merrill do lots of "little chores" that have nothing to do with selling fan belts and "motorboat gas" mixed with oil. Recently they made calls to help a stranger locate a lost relative in Adams.

"That's the way they are," says Frank Ross, the hometown guy and retired farmer who has worked at the garage since 1991. Frank's town supervisor, too.

He agrees with the twins about the town's prosperity, which may be at hand, in a modest way. The town has just about finished putting together a water district. The supervisor thinks folks will be drawing treated water from the harbor within two years.

That will stimulate settlement, he says.

"And after that, we're going for a sewer district," Frank says before he steps into the warm sunlight to answer the gas pump bell.

Still, the hamlet doesn't exactly boom just now.

"This is a village of old folks," according to Merrill's wife, Nina, who directs the choir at the United Methodist Church, Henderson's only place of worship since the Universalists closed their church. That building's now the Henderson Historical Society museum.

Nina, who used to help pump gas at the garage, would like to see more children in the pews on Sunday. She thinks the sometimes contentious merger of the Henderson and Belleville school districts 10 years ago may have cost the community young families.

Murray and Merrill love to share local history. They have stacks of historical driving tour booklets in the busy two-bay shop.

Their kin have been in Henderson for five generations. Grandfather Harley Scott farmed and lived in a landmark house he called "the stone pile." The limestone home was built by the Burnhams about 1818 and was the birthplace of Daniel Burnham, the architect credited with inventing the skyscraper.

The barn out back has two door murals by the late artist George Vander Sluis.

Nina and Merrill Scott live in the Barney House. It's said Dr. Lowery Barney had Gen. Thomas "Stonewall" Jackson and writer Edgar Allan Poe as guests there.

Merrill and Murray were drafted into World War II in their last year of high school and served in Germany in the Army Air Forces. Back home, the GI Bill and their parents saw to it the twins trained in auto mechanics at Smith Tech in Syracuse.

"After that," Merrill explains, "Dad and my brother and I formed a bond and we went into the garage business."

Except for the fact they no longer repair auto engines in motorboats, or run a tow truck, the work's pretty much the same, seven days a week with only the big holidays off. Even drivers who don't stop will wave or honk as they pass. It's that kind of place.

The twins have had a *"For Sale"* sign in the window a couple of years. They may slow down, if the right buyer is found. So far, that hasn't happened.

Their helper Frank Ross wonders if it will: "How would they keep up on what's going on all the time?"

Murray and Merrill use words of affection when they talk about their customers. Merrill spreads his arms out in an imaginary hug: "I love these people; they're family." - *2001*

Ice Storm

I've been to the dark heart of the storm.

Just then I stood in Peter Herschberger's woodworking shop on a snowy road out of Heuvelton village, in St. Lawrence County. We're a week into the national disaster that brought six counties in Northern New York to their knees.

Peter, an Amish farmer and chairmaker, hadn't missed a beat, just the way his friends in town said. He and one of his sons finished a table ordered by a customer in New Jersey.

It's past dusk and the shop's close to dark, except for the glow of a wood stove in the corner. In a bit of time, Peter has his son light two Dietz lanterns so the visiting "English" can see to talk and write things down.

The family has about 70 Dietzes handy.

Mike Davis, the mayor of Heuvelton and I interrupted the Herschbergs for a few minutes to talk about neighborliness. They're churning butter in the barn, joining wood in the shop, the way they would any day.

Amish embrace the simple life. No electric and phone lines swing into their homes to break and spark. They don't miss what they don't have.

Mike had heard the community of about 100 Amish

families in a 15-mile radius of Heuvelton had done its share, helping neighbors get around the missing pieces of their lives.

Yes, Peter's saving, that's right. But so did everybody. Don't lift us up to a special place; we're just being good neighbors.

It seemed to a visitor all of Heuvelton turned into a good neighborhood for an immense challenge. That's happened all over this ruined landscape.

I'd talked to the large-animal vet in these parts, Jack Zeh, at his house in the village. Jack's North Country; his cousin runs a dairy farm of 250 cows near Canton. He'd spent the week helping farmers save their herds.

He'd also watched his little community of 800 people come together like no one might have guessed it could.

Coming together is a way of life for his Amish neighbors, according to Jack.

"When there are hardships, your problems are everybody else's problems," he explained. "Their sense of community is so strong; like a big extended family.

"Emotionally, I think they're better off than English people. A lot of our neighbors out here are really alone, except for their immediate families."

Jack and Mike Davis said they watched as folks in their community reached out to extend the family during the storm, the way the Amish do all year.

"In the end, I was real proud of us," Mike said.

An elderly neighbor of the Hershberger's needed her

basement pumped. They did the job, using a diesel generator from the shop.

Farmers who run on electricity got behind on their milking, which they have to do, regardless. The milk they had couldn't be refrigerated; some of it had to be dumped. The Amish offered to take some, churn it and use it for their cheese.

Others gave precious water to neighbors for stock. Peter Herschberger drained his kerosene tank, sharing fuel with neighbors. He had to drive his horse and buggy into town to buy more.

No, no, he's telling Mike Davis, he never considered charging.

"You shouldn't take advantage when you're having a loss," Peter explained.

When Mike mentioned how some merchants were gouging prices for storm victims, Peter frowned. "They're asking for problems on the way home," he remarked.

Heuvelton had been looking into the mouth of this monster a week when I arrived. The village lost power Thursday, found it Monday. In between, "we threw everything into a pile and made sense of it," Mike Davis said of the community's response.

Mike grew up in Heuvelton, which sits next to the Oswegatchie River about five miles south of Ogdensburg. His dad was a cheese-maker 50 years; his mother still lives down the street.

His partners in the rescue program were Clive Chambers, the school superintendent, and Terry Harris, who is village DPW foreman and fire chief. They had a disaster drill on paper but no one had time to look at it, according to Clive's wife, Pat, the village clerk.

"I got a call from the fire department and went up and opened the school and started answering phone calls," Clive recalled. "We worked on the fly, and it came together."

The school — 750 pupils, kindergarten through high school — turned into a disaster center; the village's new fire hall down Main Street was the command center for Terry Harris and his 40 firefighters.

Firefighters handled 620 calls in the week from 20 miles around Heuvelton. One-hundred seventy-five neighbors made it to the school; the superintendent pointed out "this is the center of life in the village, anyway."

These were some of the things that helped Heuvelton get by:

School buses became taxis to pick up and move residents into the shelter.

Volunteers showed up at the school cafeteria to run a 24-hour kitchen, in shifts.

Neighbors emptied freezers and refrigerators into the school larder. The building has a large generator that runs on natural gas.

Terry and his DPW helpers kept the village water and sewage systems perking by moving generators back and forth to the plants on trucks.

People started cooking and baking on wood stoves and sharing with neighbors.

Crews were out sanding walkways.

Residents with problems were asked to signal by putting bags over their mail boxes or warning flags in the yard. There were nights the wind-chill got down to minus 45.

The Mayor and other volunteers checked each house in the village, to make sure if residents were OK or needed to go to the shelter. Only one home had serious damage; a tree crashed through the roof on the first day of the storm. The family moved next door, into the Methodist parsonage.

"Our goal was to keep as many people as possible in their homes," the mayor said. "We moved everyone from the senior center and brought in older folks and people with health problems.

"We had to do with our own food for a while. The Red Cross couldn't help; everybody was in trouble."

Heuvelton helped other communities, when it could. Early on, the village had the only reliable source of fuel, diesel and gas. Niagara Mohawk crews and other rescuers filled up. At one point, the DPW visited a nearby village to pump the fire department septic tank.

That's one reason Terry Harris got by without sleeping two days, including the times 911 went down.

At one point, with an emergency declared, Mike said he had to remind his neighbors at the shelter they couldn't leave under threat of a $1,000 fines, "and that included my mother," Betty.

The school turned out to be a perfect location for an emergency shelter. Some families got private rooms with bathrooms, in a few of the lower grade classrooms.

"They got to calling it the *'Heuvelton Hilton',*" Mike said with a laugh.

The Hilton had heat, beds, blankets, TV, good chow and entertainment.

One night, Tim Savage, the school's music director, organized a musical program in the auditorium. Other nights they were entertained by a storyteller and a guy who came in and played the piano.

The shelter also had volunteers, high school students, who looked after seniors, tucked them in at night, talked with them and swapped stories and ran messages around the community.

The mayor thought the volunteers provided their own glow in the blacked-out village.

"Everyone who worked was dirty, tired, cold and hungry but nobody complained. It was really quite a heart-warming thing to see," Mike said.

The shelter also turned into rumor central for Heuvelton.

All the unseen but very real fears huddled there. The main worry, among residents, was talk the bridge on the main drag, above the gray, roiling Oswegatchie, had given way, or was about to.

No problem, according to the DPW foreman. Even though the river rolled over a road south of town, "where it always floods," according to Terry Harris, the bridge was fine, with several gates in the Niagara Mohawk dam wide open.

"We did what we had to do to get by," Terry said. "I'm proud of our fire department."

When it came time to send people home from the shelter Monday night, the mayor and his team provided escorts. At one place, a man found his dog had frozen to death while he was gone.

"We wanted to make sure they were safe," Mike explained. "We checked on the heat and phone and provided fresh food if they needed it." Volunteers even sanded sidewalks.

Mike gathered his village board for a quick meeting Thursday afternoon. I sat in.

Heuvelton's gotten through the worst of it; now other challenges must be faced, including what Pat Chambers, the clerk, called "tons of paperwork" to document storm losses so the village gets its share of federal and state disaster money.

Heuvelton also deals with good will, which seems to be overwhelming this week. Everybody wants to help the North Country.

The village will get a hand from volunteer firefighters from Onondaga County, a work crew of state prisoners, an Ogdensburg car dealer who will lease trucks for $1 each and a group of village workers provided from outside the area by the New York State Conference of Mayors.

The board talked about helping residents get rid of some of the ice — kids are skating on front lawns on sheets several inches thick — and all those busted trees and limbs.

Mike says the state waived environmental rules for a while: the village will be able to collect and burn all that smashed pulp, which some residents already have at the curbs.

The mayor sighed: "We'll be picking up brush 'til the end of the summer."

People still need food and household goods. Donations keep coming into the town hall on Main Street; it's stacked on tables in the big room where the Lions run bingo every Thursday. Karen Cole, a nurse who lives in the village, organized a food pantry for the long haul.

The village staff also is helping residents who need prescriptions filled and other emergency medical needs.

Clive Chambers wants to start school Tuesday morning, if he can.

Meanwhile, he deals the reality of how fragile life's going to be the next few weeks.

We saw how fragile about 4:30 Thursday, when the lights went out again in Heuvelton, for about 30 minutes.

"We started getting calls from people who wondered if the shelter was going to reopen," the superintendent said later. "You know, Niagara Mohawk's told us how delicate the grid system's going to be for a while.

"That's the challenge for us, dealing with the panic. It's real, believe me." - *1998*

Up North

A cloud of warm air lifted me out of town the other day. I drifted north, toward the lake.

Winter's gone; it really is.

Moving through Oswego and Jefferson counties, all I saw in the fields were the dead ends of snow banks, butts of a long smoke ready to disappear into the water table.

Ponds and geese sit among the corn stubble.

The land is ready to feel a plow.

Our weather-maker, Lake Ontario, takes its time shaking off winter. Ice crops up on the shores in big slabs, arranged by the wind to melt into snow banks.

That's what I saw at Jefferson Park, in the town of Ellisburg: snow banks at the edge of the sand.

I saw the wind throw muddy clots of ice in waves over the banks.

I saw an empty picnic table, its legs in oozy sand. I saw two boats upside down against the bank, ready.

Our neighbors, the shore birds, are still in Florida, with the rest of the white heads. I heard a single, lonely cry as I walked down the sand. When I looked, the neighbor was gone.

I made the first set of wet shoe prints in a while. Something with wheels had been there before me.

Nobody's around, but we're not on the moon. Are we?

A wave answered.

It sent a shower of ice cubes over the bank, eating away at the birthplace of the Snow Belt, winter's last stand. In a few weeks the beach will be arranged the way we want it. June 21 is the first day of summer.

Water drips from the eaves of the camps. The shutters are down, nailed shut, some of them.

Pretty soon: sand pails, blow-up floats, fishing poles and the whishing sound a beer can makes when the top is cracked.

The big outdoor thermometer on the shed reads 42 degrees.

Back on the road north, I still haven't seen a face, except through the windshields, the young men in pickup trucks, their dogs in the passenger seats. Is everybody in Watertown? Or Tampa?

The signs are up: "*Camp Jacking.*" The vegetable stand next to the road has a snow drift on it.

Henderson Harbor's iced in.

Up the hill, in Henderson, nothing changes, praise the lord. The Scotts, Murray and Merrill, are at their Mobil station, in one of the back bays with a wheel off a truck.

The brothers are twins. They've run this landmark in their hometown almost 50 years. They know the territory.

How was winter?

Long, but not bad, according to Murray and Merrill, although a few kin and neighbors were lost.

"You know what they say," Merrill said. "'*Open winter, open graves*.'"

The interstate bridge is out at Adams. Deer are taking over the ridge above the harbor. Wild turkeys are back, all around. Sap pails are hung. The lake will be high this year.

Once, in this young springtime, it went up two feet, all of a sudden, according to the twins. Docks were riding high. Then, all of a sudden, it dropped.

The Scotts expect the ice to let go in the harbor real soon. A stiff west wind should do it.

Yep. Check the water they say and you'll know how the season goes.

What about Raquette Lake, where folks wager on the coming of spring?

I checked by phone with Ron Sharrow, who lives there, 80 miles due east of Murray and Merrill.

The lake's frozen but starting to gray up.

Folks in the western Adirondacks call Ron "The Bear." He runs South Bay Tavern at Raquette. He also runs the lake ice pool.

Neighbors place friendly bets on when lake ice leaves. It's a tradition in this mountain hamlet in Hamilton County. You wager 12-hour sections of a day, midnight till noon.

The lake breaks up in late April, the 21st to the 25th, as a rule. "Around the 25th this year," Ron predicted.

He told me on the telephone Friday that someone was pulling my leg when he told me the ice goes all at once, roaring like a Norse god. Well, yes, it did in '94, when

Raquette Lake had a windstorm.

Usually it takes a couple of days, according to Ron. Then folks know it's spring, for sure.

"Right now, there's spots where the ice is absorbing the sun's rays, starting to show through with some color," Ron explained.

Its consistency is well, sort of like, smoosch.

Smoosch, our beverage of choice for a toast to spring. - *1997*